PHILIP REMINGTON DUNN

Foreword by Craig T. Nelson

ETERNAL
JUSTICE

How God Intervenes
For the Least
of Us

FIDELIS
PUBLISHING

FIDELIS PUBLISHING

ISBN: 9-781-73662062-5
ISBN (eBook): 9-781-73662063-2

Eternal Justice
How God Intervenes for the Least of Us
© 2022 Philip Remington Dunn

Cover Design by Diana Lawrence
Interior Design by Lisa Parnell Book Services

For information about special discounts for bulk purchases, please contact BulkBooks.com, call 1-888-959-5153 or email - cs@bulkbooks.com

Fidelis Publishing, LLC Sterling, VA • Nashville, TN
fidelispublishing.com

Manufactured in the United States of America

10 9 8 7 6 5 4 3 2 1

To Rose,
my wife of noble character.

Contents

Foreword

Phil Dunn is a friend of mine, but we did not come to friendship easily. We attended the same church for ten years before we ever spoke to one another. Phil would accept responsibility for this, as he freely admits it was his pride that got in the way: "I avoid anyone who has a position of authority, particularly someone who is famous." I know better, as he is not the only one who struggles with pride.

It was his first book, *When Darkness Reigns,* which brought us together. My wife, Doria, read it and kept telling me I had to read it. Eventually she prevailed upon me, and to put it in Hollywood terms, "It knocked me out." The Holy Spirit at work in the criminal justice system . . . who would have thought it possible?

Since then, we have searched out new manifestations of the Holy Spirit together. I play the role of the mystic and Phil is the pragmatist. In our Bible study we often have different interpretations of Scripture, and after much discussion we are inevitably edified by the truth of the other's perspective. It is during our time together that I have heard many of the stories which now compile *Eternal Justice.* In so doing, Phil has taken me to places I would never have gone; he has shown me what it means to be a light shining in the darkness.

Eternal Justice is an exposé on how the Holy Spirit is vigorously manifesting Himself in the lives of the most desperate of souls. I know what it means to be "born again"—I've lived it, I have been saved by the grace of our Lord and Savior Jesus Christ. So, when I read about men like Santana Acuna, Andrew Tahmooressi, Rico Ramirez, John Jenks, and Jorge Garcia, I am reminded that we are all the same. I am no different—we all need the restoration of a loving Savior in our lives.

So many of us, even those of us so bold as to identify as Christians in these perilous times, live our lives under the influence of the mundane routine of daily existence. Its long-term effect is not unlike a narcotic stupor. We become numb to the pain of others; we disregard those souls who have strayed farthest from the path of righteousness. We forget that God loves all of us just the same. What *Eternal Justice* does is awaken us to the manifestations of a living God in our midst. A loving God, working undisguised on behalf of all of His children.

The Lord said, "I will cause all my goodness to pass in front of you, and I will proclaim my name, the LORD, in your presence. I will have mercy on whom I will have mercy, and I will have compassion on whom I will have compassion" (Exodus 33:19). By reading this book, you will find nothing has changed with our God. He still lights our path with goodness and proclaims His name in our presence. I urge you: take the journey, experience all the mercy and compassion of our God, and discover how His purpose is being fulfilled to this day.

Yours in Christ,
Craig T. Nelson

Preface

Does God intervene in our lives? If so, why does God so often seem to ignore our prayers? There have been countless scholars throughout the ages who have attempted various answers to this most significant question. Thus, the issue isn't new, but as old as the Bible. It was certainly true for Job, and David perhaps said it best, "My God, my God, why have you forsaken me? Why are you so far from saving me, so far from the cries of anguish?" (Psalm 22:1).

Yet, as Christians we believe God does intervene in our lives. We have faith. Is that faith based merely upon what we believe, or is it also based upon experience? Certainly, the Bible provides countless examples of God's intervention on behalf of His people, those reported in Exodus being perhaps the most vivid. Then there is the ultimate intervention in human history, the redeeming sacrifice of God's only Son, Jesus Christ. But the question still lingers, does God intervene in our lives today?

This book offers no new or more profound theological understanding of this ultimate question. Rather, it offers evidence, what a trial lawyer such as myself might call *experiential evidence.* Eight true stories about real people for whom God undeniably intervened.

Why God chose to intervene in these individuals' lives, and perhaps not others, I will leave to God. "I will put my trust in him" (Hebrews 2:13). God's timing and purposes may at times appear arbitrary to us mere mortals, but that in no way diminishes the occasions in which He acts in miraculous ways. He is God, and we are not.

My own experience with God's intervention is what led me to this place of understanding. It occurred when I was a young man filled with ambition and promise. I had just completed a harrowing three years of law school, where my feet were kept to the fire of failure throughout my tenure. Of the original class of about three hundred, fewer than two hundred made it to graduation. I was blessed with Rose, my wife, who not only sustained me, but supported us both throughout the grind. While studying for the Bar, we were further blessed by the birth of Rebecca, our first child. Having passed the California Bar exam, I was a newly minted lawyer coming online in the midst of a recession.

I wanted to be a trial attorney, as that was where my gifts resided at the time, and to fulfill my ambition—and an almost psychopathic need to win—I knew I wanted to become a deputy district attorney (DDA). I managed to get an interview with the Ventura County district attorney's office, which was my dream job as it would allow me to return to the community in which I grew up. Seeking any advantage, the morning of the interview I went to my knees asking for God's intervention on my behalf. In a moment of humility born of fear, I concluded my prayer with, "Not my will, but Your will be done."

As far as I could tell, the interview went well, but I was disappointed to learn their process might take six months. I needed a job right away, as we left Rose's good job behind, and risked it all on my future prospects. Walking in I noticed the public defender's office was on the second floor right below the DA's office. I knew a starting position with either office paid the same. Feeling a little desperate, I went résumé in hand into the PD's office. I walked to the front desk and was received by a matronly woman who upon introduction told me, "I'm Mr. Erwin's personal secretary, filling in up front today, and you know what, sometimes he'll see young men like you right away, if you want take a seat and see when he might be available."

"Yes please, I'll wait as long as it takes." She left out the back door as I turned to have a seat among the clients awaiting interviews with their lawyers. They were not what I expected. I imagined serious criminal types, the ones I envisioned prosecuting. Rather, they looked young, poor, and anxious. Many sat with their parents, whose discomfort was evident. My reaction surprised me even more, perhaps best described as empathy. As I would soon discover, this was not a healthy emotion for someone who wished to be a prosecutor.

The door to the reception area swung open as Mr. Erwin's secretary, Eileen was her name, walked through and said, "Follow me, Mr. Dunn, Mr. Erwin will see you now."

Richard Erwin's office was spacious, with one side a window looking out upon a courtyard view of the surrounding

grounds of a modern criminal justice complex. Two other lawyers sat in the back listening with obvious amusement as Mr.
Erwin engaged in a tirade about "those damn municipal court
judges." He motioned for me to have a seat as he gave instructions to the others: "I want you to file a writ with the superior
court—they're not going to get away with this one."

As Mr. Erwin continued with some of the finer points of
his writ, I was able to observe the man in his environment.
Better than six feet, thin build, white hair, and thick wire-
rimmed glasses, he looked past seventy. No shortage of passion,
however; he was the definition of zealous advocacy. Dressed
entirely in black, string tie, and a black cowboy hat hanging from a hat rack, he embodied the rural roots of Ventura
County. His desk was large for government issue, festooned
with legal briefs and various mementos of a stellar legal career.
This was further supported by his back wall covered in plaques
and degrees awarded by various legal societies and universities.

As Mr. Erwin concluded his tutorial, the other lawyers
made their way out of the office, but not before giving me the
once-over. "So young man, what's makes you think you might
be a trial attorney someday?"

The old man's earlier diatribe put me at ease. It felt as if I
was a privileged recruit listening to Knute Rockne inspire his
team to victory. "Well, sir, it would seem you're having trouble
with some of your judges, but it's your jurors I'm interested in,
what are they like?"

I could tell I'd asked the right question as he leaned forward, putting his elbows on the desk and clasping his hands.
"They're good folk, a lot of farmers with manure on their
boots, but honest, hard-working people."

"Seems to me they decide the guilt or innocence of your clients—they're the ones I want a shot at." Once again it seemed I'd given the right answer. He looked me up and down before saying, "Alright then, I guess Eileen's got your résumé, she'll let you know if we got anything else for you." My interview was over; I saw myself out of his office.

As soon as I got home, I began describing to Rose my interview with the DA's office. I hadn't gotten far before we were interrupted by the phone. Rose answered, looking confused; she finally put her hand over the receiver: "It's Eileen, she says she's calling for a Mr. Erwin?" I jumped to my feet to grab the phone to mutter, "Hello."

"Hold on, Mr. Erwin will be right with you."

"Young man, the doors open at 8:15, if you want a job, show up ready to go tomorrow morning."

"Yes, sir, I'll be there."

It took me a while to explain who Eileen and Mr. Erwin were, but when I finished, Rose could not have been happier. Her heart has always been with the underdog, and it was a county paycheck.

Thirty-four years later I can honestly say God knew me better than I knew myself. It certainly hasn't been easy, and I knew I was setting aside ambitions of professional status and power, but I wouldn't trade a moment. If for no other reason than my career became my mission field.

I started out in arraignment court. It was the best place to learn the ropes as every day thirty or forty new cases came in. My job was to make the best deal I could for them, and if it wasn't good enough, I would set their case for trial. I loved the give and take of plea bargaining with the judge and the

DDA. It is a remarkable commitment to justice for each individual caught up in the criminal justice system, that they are assigned a lawyer paid for by the county, if they cannot afford one. Public defenders balance the scales of justice, without them the power of the law enforcement juggernaut would be unstoppable. But, as one judge once told a jury of mine, "You know, Mr. Dunn, we didn't just pick your client's name out of a hat."

It is true most of the clients are guilty of something, but not all, and not of everything they are charged with. Even so, the clients are in the system for a reason, and most often it involves addiction of one sort or another. Whether legal or illegal drugs, DUI, or the violence so often fueled by intoxication, addiction is invariably at the heart of criminal conduct. This tragic reality soon caused disillusionment, as I came to grips with the revolving door of the criminal justice system. I'd get a client out of jail one day, and a week later he'd be back in for the same thing. "Once a heroin addict, always a heroin addict. Phil, get used to it." This was the advice of another judge, given as I expressed my frustration at having to represent the same client, for the same crime, multiple times.

Then one day I noticed a Hispanic gentleman in a three-piece suit sitting in the gallery of my courtroom. About my age, dark hair, large brush mustache—I couldn't help but notice him as he obviously was not one of the clients. He came back the next day, and the next, always sitting up front. Finally, at the end of the third day I approached him, "I'm Phil Dunn with the PD's office, couldn't help but notice you sitting here for the last three days." I extended my hand; he shook it firmly.

"I'm Pastor Bob Herrera of the Victory Outreach Church of Ventura County."

"You've been sitting here for three days. What's up with that?"

"I'm waiting for that judge to sentence one of these men to my rehabilitation home, instead of jail."

"You know someone in custody, a specific case?"

"No, I'm just acting on faith, waiting for the Lord to move the judge's heart."

"Well, you may wait a long time for that with Judge 'Hang 'em High' Hunter."

Pastor Bob wasn't amused by my cynicism. His faith was absolute, a man on a mission from God. "I don't know how long it will take, but I'm going to keep showing up, until it happens."

Intrigued, amused, inspired, I don't know which one—perhaps all three, but I took a chance. "You know I'm done with the calendar for today, you got time for a cup of coffee?"

"You bet."

It was a short walk to the courthouse cafeteria. I soon learned Victory Outreach was a nondenominational church in most every inner city in the United States. Started by Pastor Sonny Arguinzoni, a former heroin addict, who was discipled by David Wilkerson, founder of Teen Challenge, and author of *The Cross and the Switchblade*, a book I read as a youth. Bob told me their mission statement was "taking treasures out of darkness."

"You need to see our 'Men's Home.' I've got eight men in their now, felons on parole, drug addicts, homeless taken off the streets, all learning about the love Jesus has for them."

"I just might take you up on that sometime," and I did. I even took a judge with me—Burt Henson, who I knew to be a born-again Christian. To say we were moved by what we heard and saw would be an understatement. Bob lived in one of the roughest neighborhoods in Ventura County, just off Ventura Avenue in the City of Ventura.

"When I came to Ventura, I drove around looking for the place that had the most graffiti," he told us. He landed in a three-bedroom house with his wife and four children, all under the age of six. The garage was his Men's Home. Eight men lived there sleeping in four bunk bed sets. "We start at six in the morning with prayer and Bible study, then if we got a job, we go work it, if not they help out around the house. After dinner we do another Bible study, then lights out."

One by one each man came forward and stood before the little pulpit Bob set up in his garage. Each testimony started with "I would like to thank my Lord and Savior Jesus Christ for my salvation." Then, we got each man's life story, the abuse he suffered as a child, when he started drinking and doing drugs, why he joined the local street gang, how much time he did in jail, prison, or on the streets. To graduate you had to stay sober and go through the entire Bible in a year. The judge and I were in tears by the time the last man finished, so moved were we by the hope and courage we witnessed. It changed everything for me, so much so, when I got a call from the DA's office offering me a position, I told them, "I'm already playing for the Raiders, I don't want to play for the Patriots."

This was my first step in a lifelong pilgrimage. I soon developed a strong friendship with Pastor Bob, and whenever he had a new man enter the men's home with pending charges,

I represented him. Judge Henson told the other judges about Pastor Bob and his Christian rehabilitation home. It was always a struggle, and the DA always objected, but I can no longer count the number of men and women for whom I got an alternative sentence of a year in the Victory Outreach Christian Rehabilitation Home, instead of jail or prison. The vast majority of them stayed sober, became solid citizens, and best of all, missionaries sent back into their communities.

Recent academic studies on mass incarceration and abysmally high recidivism rates of paroled inmates from American prisons provide proof that my anecdotal evidence is sound. In an October 2021 article in *Christianity Today*—"The New Prison Ministry Lies in Bible Education"—put it this way:

> Faith-based programs are successful in reducing recidivism. . . . Over the past several decades an entire research literature has emerged confirming the positive and prosocial effects of religion on crime reduction and restorative justice approaches.[1]

Ultimately, this is the only hope for turning around a societal catastrophe spawned by a criminal justice system discouraging the moral rehabilitation of those incarcerated souls who most desperately need it.

I could only withstand the constrictions of government employment for three years. I then went into private practice which gave me greater freedom to pick and choose my clients, and how I represented them. My approach to criminal defense became holistic in nature. That is, I not only sought to set the body free, but also the mind. Criminal behavior is simply that sin which society has decided must be punished in order to protect itself. Recognizing this fact provides hope of spiritual redemption. The redeeming power of our Lord and Savior Jesus Christ works in real life, even among the most desperately lost souls. I have personally witnessed it, and I can testify it is true, and I am not alone in that conclusion.

As my faith journey progressed, I ventured into other arenas. So, the following stories are not only tales drawn out of the criminal justice system, but also other places where people are in severe distress. Places like the poorest neighborhoods of Mexico, prisons in El Salvador, Mexico and the United States, the jungles of Columbia, combat zones from foreign and domestic battles, and most significantly; the soul residing within each of us. It is here, as Solzhenitsyn reminds us, where the battle line between good and evil runs through the heart of every human being.[2]

It is in these places I have experienced God's intervention. I suppose one could discount the miraculous nature of these events, as mere coincidences and/or a testament to the power of the human spirit. Perhaps taken in isolation I might submit to such a rationalization. But, for this observer, the character and content of these events, and the miraculous transformations of the individuals described lead to only one possible conclusion. God intervened in their lives at a critical moment, or as Jesus told us, He brought down the kingdom of God "on earth as it is in heaven" (Matthew 6:10).

CHAPTER ONE

Santana's Last Stand

It should have been his last stand. Respected for his courage and brutality, Santana Acuna should have welcomed a proper outlaw ending. Barricaded inside a house, hostages taken, guns drawn, countless patrol cars lighting up the night, the timing was perfect. But once again, it was taking control, it was overpowering his will and stealing his strength . . . the Carga—smack, heroin. He still had some and it would once again take his dignity. Worse, it would take his manhood.

It was George who got him here. George, the father of his grandchildren, George had no respect. Santana may have been named for the "Devil Wind" and lived up to that name his whole life, but George was too stupid to know who he was messing with. So stupid he beat up Santana's daughter. So stupid, high, and drunk he called Santana out in the middle of the night in front of the whole neighborhood. The last time George acted this stupid they were doing time together at San Quentin. The only thing that saved him then was a couple of "homies" who convinced Santana, George was so stupid—he didn't even know he was stupid.

Drunk on whiskey and high on heroin, Santana finally had enough of George's tough-guy act. He got up, loaded his .22, went outside and started blasting. The shots hit George three times, the last one in the leg, sending him to the ground. Santana ran to where he lay, put the barrel to his head, but he didn't pull the trigger—he spit in his face instead; a big mistake. George talked to the police. He was a punk-ass snitch.

It was the same with Pablo—big talk, no respect. Don't be talking smack about Santana in the neighborhood. Santana shot him ten times, and Pablo must have made it because the cops knew where to find him. Santana should have taken off out the back door like the other homies, but he didn't. He couldn't leave without grabbing his stash first. Now the police had the place surrounded.

Oh well, thought Santana, he still had his Carga and he wasn't going anywhere until it was gone. He got the kit out, cooked it up, and stuck the needle in his arm.

In that moment, it was all worth it. He sold, pimped, and robbed for this high for more than thirty years. Since his first taste at sixteen, it defined him in every way. No longer a proud outlaw in the tradition of Pancho Villa, he was a slave to master heroin. It owned him.

There were kids in the house under the bed in the back bedroom. He knew it was the only reason they were still calling, asking him to surrender instead of just breaking in with guns blazing. The negotiator called and Santana told him he would only surrender to the chief of police, no one else. That should take a while, to wake his ass up and get him over here. Still, this meant prison—again. Even worse, this meant withdrawal—cold turkey—inside that concrete cage. The shaking, sweating, wanting to peel your skin off, it was a hell only a true addict could understand. Just the thought of it made him want to die. Maybe it was better to die right here, quickly?

Prison again, just the thought kills my high. What did I go for last time? Oh yeah, the old man in the bathroom.

« « » »

Somebody shot at him from a car while he was walking down the street.

Enraged and disrespected, Santana had to strike back. He thought he knew the neighborhood they were from, and the Mexican restaurant where they all hung out—whisky had his courage up. When he got there, the only ones there were part of a wedding party. Drunk as he was, he called them out anyway. An old guy in a tuxedo answered the call telling him to leave. "No, I won't get 'out of here.' I'll see you in the bathroom!" He walked in, combed his hair, and felt for the lead pipe in his pocket.

The old man burst in swinging, nicking him on the jaw. As Santana pivoted, he grabbed the pipe and came down full force on the man's forehead. Warm blood splattered on his hands. The old man staggered backward.

Defenseless, Santana took another swing, hitting him on the side of the head, the blow sounded like a hammer hitting wood.

The old man dropped to his knees, blood rivered down his face, the pipe was getting sticky in Santana's hand. A straight overhand to the back of the head, the pipe lodged in the old man's skull. Blood lust now ruled Santana. Dropping a knee on the fallen man's back, he struck him again and again, back and forth, over and over. He couldn't stop. Blood covered his hands, his clothes, and even misted his face red.

His primeval scream of triumph echoed off the walls. Throwing the pipe to the ground, Santana stood over his vanquished foe and spit in his face.

The old man didn't move. The only sign of life was the flow of red pulsating into a pool beneath him. Having been here before, Santana searched for the pipe, found it, and made for the door. Hitting it with the palm of his hand, he left behind identifying evidence. Outside, no one waited for him. The old man was alone, no gangsta' jump for him. Santana didn't run, he walked upright, pushing his way through wedding guests. He glanced back to see two younger men head into the bathroom. As he reached the front door a woman's scream silenced the party. He turned back to see two women, both in bridal dresses—one older, the other clearly the bride—put their hands to their faces. Both dissolved into shrieks of grief as they looked in upon their fallen husband and father.

Santana got away, but not for long. Arrested for assault with a deadly weapon, three weeks later the old man died in the hospital. Murder. Santana was facing life in prison.

« « » »

Sitting in jail, the agony came upon him. Pain without injury, the synapses in his brain screamed for the substance they became dependent upon. Like the flu but much worse. Profuse sweating, shaking so severely he could not stand.

The first three days are the worst, and then the physical symptoms diminish, but the craving for the high never goes away. Rage replaced pain.

≪ ≪ ≫ ≫

His prosecutor was a wimp. Lazy, he didn't want to go to trial on a self-defense case. It was mutual combat after all; everyone saw the old man go in the bathroom looking for a fight. He could have had a knife or even a gun. Santana couldn't take that chance. Kill or be killed. Just might sell it to a jury, DA offered him a manslaughter charge. He took it, got a sentence of ten to life, and got out in six.

He didn't wait a day; he was right back at it. "Friends" fixed him up. High on heroin, drunk on whiskey, he needed a woman. Anything for Santana, the shot caller was back in town. It wouldn't last; he had to pay his own way. Getting back into the drug trade was easy, but it couldn't sustain his lifestyle. An armed robbery now and then covered his over-head. It was working, until George and Pablo started acting stupid.

≪ ≪ ≫ ≫

The sound of a car pulling up and doors slamming propelled Santana back to the present. Peeking through the blinds, he could see Robert Smith, chief of police, standing just outside the front gate. Now it was a matter of honor. Santana said he'd surrender to the chief, and the chief was here. "Honor among thieves," even outlaw gangsters believed in something. It was time to give it up. Let's get it over with.

Santana opened the door, showed his hands first, and walked out into the blinding light. They were on him in an instant, straight to the ground, knee in the back, first one wrist cuffed, then the other. Game over.

Slammed down in a cell with his heroin high fading, Santana slipped into a rare moment of self-reflection. *How did I get here?* He thought of his father, a migrant farm worker who came down with pneumonia, but kept working. *Died ten days before I was born. Mi madre couldn't do it alone, left me with Abuela Juanita. That was good though; she loved me like her own. But she also loved her wine, sometimes a gallon a day. She shared it with me.*

Santana never went to school, but his abuela didn't think he needed it. She told him, "By ten you'll be in the fields anyway." But at nine, his mother came back for him. She married Don Pancho, a hardened man who worked the vineyards of La Misión. From the beginning, he let it be known, "I will break you to my ways." This meant heavy labor—chopping wood, shoveling manure, and working the fields. If not done to his liking, Santana was whipped with a belt or beaten with a stick.

"My mother never said a word, afraid for herself and her other children," Santana explained. "As I grew, my anger grew, first with plans of revenge, with each new beating my rage turned into hatred, I knew my day would come."

"He had no reason to beat me the last time, he just liked it. One time I got to the stick first, got him right above the eye." Don Pancho fell back, blood seeping into his eyes.

"He left me alone after that." He learned the power of fear. Fear of the wild animal, respect earned through violence.

"Respect meant freedom, freedom to do and take what I wanted. Little things first; some other kids' lunch, then his shoes, maybe some money. If the older boys picked on me, I'd go crazy. Pick up a rock, any kind of weapon. Before long I carried a knife, and then my .38. It cost me a month in the fields, but it was worth it. Power, I held death in my hand.

"Come to think of it, that was about the time I met Carga—the two went together. The one fed and protected the other. It's also when I started getting arrested. Juvenile hall first; it wasn't so bad. I was safe for a while, made new friends, bandits like me. Then jail, not good when I was young, they were just starting to gang up in those days. They'd make you join, jump you, there were too many; you couldn't fight them all. Got hurt a few times; hurt them too, until they finally moved on to weaker boys. I got a rep as a fighter, an outlaw—they called me, 'El Santana.'"

« « » »

Dread invaded Santana's mind. *Withdrawal, it's inevitable. No appetite, hate the jail slop anyway, but the first symptom? No, not yet, but soon.* Santana struggled to remember anything good, a place in his mind to hide from the terror he knew was coming.

There was a time, when the Ramirezes came to La Misión. *They were kind, I played with their kids and I didn't want to go home. They fed me, took me to church. First communion, confession, they were so proud of me.*

"God? Who is that?" Santana startled himself, his voice bounced off the concrete walls. "God! You help everyone else, why not help me? Why don't you save me from the pain, I can't do this anymore!" Tears, streamed down his cheeks. Shame first, then fear. *No, it's okay, no one's here to see me.* More tears, dropping to the cement below. Never before—maybe as a baby—can't stand, must be the shakes already—too early.

Santana fell into the steel bed, curled up like a child, and wept. Exhaustion, his sobs finally fading away. Peace, as sleep came upon him.

I remember getting up a few times, going to the john, eating a couple of cheese sandwiches and an old apple.

"Hey! You alive in there," the jailers voice came through the mesh in the steel door.

"Huh, ahhhh yeah, I guess so?"

"It's Thursday, man, you've hardly moved for three days."

Santana heard boots on cement fading away as the jailer moved on.

"Three days, no way, I'd be sick by now," he said to no one.

Santana felt hunger—the smell of overcooked spaghetti coming from the door. *I shouldn't eat. I'll just get sick, but I'm hungry? I don't understand.* He went to the door, grabbed the tray and plastic fork; ate it all.

No pain, I feel good, strong even, not possible . . . Then he remembered his plea. *Prayer, I don't know how to pray.* The mystery of it all frightened him, but it was real. Gone was the dread, comfort reigned in his healthy body. Peace replaced sorrow; the sickness was gone.

"God answered my prayer," he spoke softly to himself in disbelief. *I'm not sick. I'm not going to get sick; it can't be.* The moment brought Santana to his knees; he no longer felt alone, someone was looking after him. *I feel at peace—no, more than that—I feel loved.*

Tears flowed again, not from desperation, but from joy. *God heard me, He answered my prayer, He will look after me, I don't have to be afraid any more.*

There is no telling how long Santana stayed on his knees, sharing his thoughts with the God who heard him. Eventually, he made his way back to the mattress, settled in, and slept like he'd never slept before. When Santana finally awoke, he knew what he had to do. If God was being straight with him, he'd do the same. He called for the jailer.

"Hey boss, I want to confess," he said when the jailer arrived.

"I'm not your detective; I don't have time for this."

"No, I mean it, please bring me paper and pen—" Santana caught himself, *I said please . . . to a jailer, no less.*

"Alright man, but this better be real."

Santana wrote it out, every single detail. He knew it was stupid . . . felony stupid. *I'll get life for sure, but it had to end someday.* Within an hour his detective was there.

"Here it is," Santana told him, "but I'll only sign it in front of the judge." Two hours later he was in a courtroom.

"Mr. Acuna, do you freely confess to these crimes?" the judge asked, unsure of what to make of Santana's dramatic change of heart.

"Yes, sir," he replied as sincerely as he'd ever been.

"You do know if you plead guilty, straight up, no deal, I could give you—let's see, close to a hundred years. You understand that?"

"Yes, sir," Santana replied, knowing exactly what the judge meant. He lived his entire life dealing with the penal code. He knew there was no going back, he was giving his life over to a judge. The judge in the courtroom, or the judge of the Universe, it didn't matter. Santana was compelled to speak the truth.

"Mr. Acuna, I can see here you've been around the block more than once, your record is about as bad as it gets: state prison three, four times; drugs, armed robbery, assault, manslaughter. You deserve a hundred years."

"Yes, sir."

"So why are you doing this?"

"I believe in God now," Santana replied. Calmness settled over him just saying the words. "I have to follow God. I need to tell the truth, and trust in Him. I'm not afraid of what's going to happen anymore."

Silence. The uncomfortable kind came over the courtroom as the judge deliberated. Finally, the faint sound of pen to paper—a calculation being made—then he spoke. "Alright, Mr. Acuna. I accept your plea of guilty as to each and every count, and to those various counts I sentence you to an indeterminate term in the department of corrections of eleven to seventeen years. There being no further business before the court, bailiff remand the prisoner back into custody, and with that this court's adjourned."

Santana said nothing, too stunned to speak. He stood passively, looking at the judge's bench as the man stepped down and went out the back door to his chambers.

"Let's go," came the command of the bailiff, grabbing Santana's belly chain from behind. Santana walked slowly back through the custody door, his steps shortened by the shackles around his ankles.

Did I hear that right . . . eleven to seventeen? I'm going to get out someday?!

First Chino, then Soledad, but this time it had to be different. No more drugs, no more vendettas, no respect. As soon as the homies know I don't fight no more, it will be trouble. They'll try me. They'll want to take "El Santana" down.

It didn't take long before he got tested. A homie from the neighborhood walked up to him on the yard, shook his hand, and pressed a bundle of heroin into it, "Welcome back, *carnale.*"

Santana knew what it was, but couldn't give it back, he couldn't "disrespect the man." Instead, he sold it for five bucks. It didn't seem right. What does it mean to be a man of God? Is it possible on the inside?

Slowly, Santana's carnales began to realize he was different, and not everyone liked it. "Going soft" often meant relying on the guards for protection. Prison gangs enforce harsh discipline on fellow prisoners for all kinds of infractions, such as talking with a man of another race. The most ruthless assaults however, were reserved for "snitches." Slowly, rumor spread that Santana must be snitching.

"I started reading the Bible every night, writing out verses and memorizing them. I went to a Bible study; the brothers were shocked to see me. At first, they didn't trust me, but they amazed me. Men of different races would sit together, talk, laugh, shake each other's hands, even hug. That took some getting used to.

"Outside the chapel, we really couldn't talk, but inside we were all brothers in Christ. I learned from these men, I learned life could be different, even on the inside.

I wanted to be a part of them, and what they were doing. I told them I wanted to be baptized."

Baptisms in prison are like nowhere else. It's not as if a baptismal is available, or a swimming pool, but fortunately inmates do have a constitutional right to practice their religion; thus, accommodations have to be made. Usually that comes in the form of a large trash dumpster—filled with water to the brim. This is how Santana was baptized. A garbage can filled with water, surrounded by his fellow inmates—now his brothers. It was a glorious moment. He made a public proclamation of his faith; he chose to fulfill his commitment to God. His brothers in Christ rejoiced, knowing even the most wicked of men could be redeemed. He spent thirty-four years working for evil, now Santana went over to the other side.

Challenges still abounded in his life, and his anger sometimes got the best of him, but he learned Christians aren't perfect. As he forgave others, he accepted forgiveness himself. It didn't happen overnight, but out of respect for his new way of life, and his sincere desire to be a new man, his old friends, the big homies, largely left him alone.

Time passed quickly, more peaceably, this go-around. After six years he was again eligible for parole. Since he became a model prisoner, in spite of his record, he was released.

≪ ≪ ≫ ≫

Going home was dangerous. He knew the temptations of his former life were powerful, particularly the first day out. "Nothing like that first heroin high, after six years clean, it can't be described. Shoot up, find a woman, there were still twenty-year olds available to me."

Fortunately for Santana, he had a friend on the outside. His name was Pastor Frank, from "Soldiers for Christ" ministry. He visited and wrote to Santana for months prior to his release. Pastor Frank picked him up the day he was paroled.

They drove through his old neighborhood, just the sight of it made his pulse rise, how easy he could score some Carga.

The sight of a woman crossing the street made his palms sweat. For the last five years Santana lived like a monk in a monastery, now the world came rushing back into his consciousness. He made a commitment, a personal covenant with God: *I will not go back to inflicting pain and terror on those around me, or myself.*

"With the same determination that supported a heroin habit for thirty-four years—for which I robbed, shot, and stabbed people—I now dedicated myself to saving others from the misery I had known for so long."

When the car finally stopped, he was at Pastor Frank's Home of the Redeemed. He would share a room with five other men: drug addicts, convicted felons, the homeless, and the hopeless. Pastor Frank turned away no one. He fed, clothed, sheltered, and preached to them. Santana finally found a home.

The first night he couldn't sleep. Filled with anxiety and self-doubt, he went outside. *Being an outlaw is all I know, how can I ever do anything right, be good to anyone?* Then it came to him, he knew what he had to do. He went to the chapel to pray. On his knees before the altar, in anguish, he again pleaded for God's intervention in his life. The answer was already within him, a verse he memorized:

> "For I know the plans I have for you," declares the LORD, "plans to prosper you and not to harm you, plans to give you hope and a future." (Jeremiah 29:11).

Santana's covenant with God was renewed.

« « » »

Pastors like Frank and their ministries are common in urban centers of America. They receive little recognition and no government support, but they do an enormous public service. In California for instance, 25 percent of paroled inmates are homeless when they leave prison. The $200 they're given upon release doesn't last long, so desperation sets in quickly. The sanctuary offered by these ministries provides an alternative to a life of crime.

These men needed the discipline of study and sober living. For the first sixty days they were not allowed to leave the home. Churches donated food and clothing, individual gifts paid the rent, and sometimes a special meal was prepared at the home of a local believer. Santana looked forward to the nights when the men piled into the two aging vans and went out for a home-cooked meal. Oftentimes they had little more than rice, beans, and tortillas at the home. This tested Santana, as an outlaw he could afford the best restaurants; he wasn't used to living humbly.

On one occasion they were invited to the home of Sister Rose and her daughter Emma.

« « » »

Entering the small, neatly kept home, the men caught the aroma of a Mexican feast in the making. Skirt steak, pulled pork, shredded chicken, tamales, enchiladas, refried beans, rice, fried vegetables, and freshly chopped salsa. But before they could eat, they had to endure another sermon from Pastor Frank.

As Pastor Frank spoke on and on, the two women worked in the kitchen. When the sermon finally ended, the women moved to a far corner of the living room, sat down, and picked up their knitting. The men got in line to serve themselves and then found a place at the table. Santana chose a spot that happened to face Sister Rose and her daughter seated at the opposite side of the room. The air was festive. The men talked freely and ate ravenously.

Santana, on the other hand, grew still. He ate nothing. He couldn't take his eyes off Sister Rose. Across the dimly lit room he noticed her look up from her knitting, catching his eyes, her gaze quickly returned to her hands. Emma, on the other hand, never looked up.

I've seen her before. She's older now, with thick glasses, gray hair, but that face . . . I remember it. No—not just Rose. Her daughter too—a pretty little thing, light skin, with jet-black hair and soft brown eyes. Did I know her? No, not like that.

The memory is dark, tragic, horrible—No! Oh my God, NO! It can't be, but yes, it's them! It's the mother and daughter from the wedding. The wife of the old man—dear God, he was the father of the bride. She was the bride. I beat him with a pipe. It took him a month to die. I saw them crying, crippled by my rage, destroyed by my evil, it can't be true, it can't be them, but it is . . . I am in their house, they're feeding me . . .

They must not know who I am.

Maybe if I keep cool, stay at the back of the room, slide out the side door . . .

Sister Rose looked up, caught his eyes again, and didn't look away. Santana looked away in terror.

She knows! My God she knows it's me! How is that possible, no! It can't be.

Santana gathered his courage. Looking up he caught her gaze again. He saw no anger, no hate, acknowledgment nonetheless. Sister Rose knew. She knew it was Santana—"El Santana," that evil, horrific man who beat her husband to death.

What do I do? How can I stay here, sit here?

All the muscles in his body tightened. Palms flat on the table, he pushed so hard the solid oak table slid away, startling the other men seated there. He was standing, head down, he moved toward her. Tears ran warm down his cheeks. Silence, everyone watching him.

I can't go on . . . Yet somehow, he shuffled his way across the room, never once taking his eyes off the floor. Sister Rose and Emma waited for him, as if they knew he would come. Frozen in time, they remained transfixed upon him.

As he got close, Emma faltered, sliding back in her chair, she turned away in fear. Sister Rose didn't blink, her eyes remained fixed upon him. Santana fell to his knees before her. He quivered as he tried to raise his head to speak, to say something, anything, but he could not. There were no words, nothing, just more tears.

She touched him, gently stroking his head. Softly caressing his hair, it gave him the strength to look up into her eyes. Compassion was all he could see, a kindness he could not imagine.

"Santana, 'El Santana,' did you not know—that I—we—forgave you long ago."

He would later describe the moment: "I heard myself sobbing, like I wasn't there, this couldn't be me, but it was. I was broken, and yet I felt safe for the first time in my life. A miracle had cleansed me, a miracle of love, unconditional love for me."

«« »»

Santana remembers little about how he left Sister Rose's that night, but what he does remember is the change started within him years earlier and was now complete. He would go on to graduate from the program, and Pastor Frank made him its spiritual leader.

"I cried before men again, but without fear this time. It may not seem like a big deal, but it was everything to me. It was the first good thing I had ever done in my life."

He became an ordained pastor with a local ministry called Soldiers for Christ. Placed in charge of three homes, he spent many sleepless nights nursing drug addicts through the agony of withdrawal. All the cruelty left him, leaving behind a kind and gentle man.

For those who knew the outlaw, the change was suspect, and not always welcome. Even his children weren't sure of him. Decades of crime and punishment were not so easily washed away. Of his six children (by three different women), two of his boys followed in his footsteps, and two of the girls struggled as well. Santana Jr. went to prison for life, and Santanilla also did time. Gangbanging invaded their neighborhood, and his boys jumped right in. Time in prison was a badge of honor in the barrio. The sins of the father passed down to his children, and then his grandchildren.

"I blame myself; they followed my example. Going bad is quick and easy; doing good is hard work and slow. But the girls have come around, I like to think the change in me had something to do with that."

Over time, Santana's life as a pastor blossomed. The story of his transformation had no equal in evangelical circles. The small church he started grew into a force for revival in the community. His reputation remained, but his new life inspired others to get clean and change their lives.

Santana made new friends, even an old "acquaintance," Bill Tell. After a career in law enforcement, Bill also became a pastor. He asked Santana to give his testimony one Sunday at his church in San Bernardino. Afterward, he told Santana of their previous contact.

"Bill told me, 'I was a sharpshooter with the Sheriff's Department called out to a hostage situation. I set up on the trunk of the car with orders to shoot the hostage taker if I had a clear shot. Good thing you surrendered to the chief when you did, the way you were moving around in there; it was just a matter of time.'"

« « » »

When I first met Santana, his face still bore the scars of countless battles, his flesh tone the dark pigment of Oaxaca ancestry. Perhaps five-eight, but still sculpted by decades of working out on the yard. His hair and brush mustache, dyed jet black, made him look younger than his seventy years. Slammed down for more than twenty-six years, he still carried himself like the "shot caller" he once was. A made member of the Mexican Mafia, he appreciated that I knew a "tax collector" got payment from local drug dealers. I knew he carved on his body the needle and pen ink tattoo of an Aztec warrior, the ultimate symbol of respect—both in prison or on the streets—but none were visible. Now he covered his tats with a long sleeve button-down shirt commonly worn by *cholos* in the 'hood. He received permission to "drop out," having proven his conversion sincere. "Even the worst of the worst have the right to save their own soul." They let him go, Santana was no longer a puppet controlled by the strings of evil.

Oh yeah, Santana was the real deal, I'd represented enough serious gangsters in my time to know the difference. Rarely did he reveal a hint of emotion, rather he listened more than he spoke, carefully sizing me up before revealing anything about himself.

I started with his ministry; of this he spoke freely. Working my way backward, I got his history: brutal childhood, countless crimes, years in prison all the way through to his conversion. Sister Rose and her daughter Emma were a tougher sell. For the first time, pain passed through his eyes. I told the story, he listened; I asked for confirmation, he hesitated.

"That is still a problem for me. Bringing it up might hurt someone."

"Who?" I asked.

"Her family, not everyone is so forgiving. They don't understand."

"You mean Sister Rose?"

"Yes, but others too."

"Can I meet her?"

"I don't know, I'd have to ask. Why? Why do you want to meet her?" He was still sizing me up.

"The truth. I want to know if it's true; I have to hear it from her."

With that, Santana nodded in acknowledgment. The Truth. The words resonated with him.

"I visit her every week in the rest home. She's on dialysis now, not doing so good, but still all there."

"Tell me about that." I was fascinated by this woman I had never met.

"Well, I'm a pastor now, that's what we do."

My skeptical look must have encouraged him because he continued. "It's hard to understand, but we are close now, she calls me *mijo*."

Once again doubt invaded my mind. Forgiveness was one thing; treating him like a son another.

"Will you ask for me, see if I can meet her?"

"We'll see . . ." he replied. I would have to wait.

≪ ≪ ≫ ≫

It was many months before it was arranged. I told the story to my pastor, Michael Mudgett, who was equally amazed and wanted to see for himself, so together we went. We met Santana in the lobby of the nursing home and he led us to her room. Walking the corridors brought back unpleasant memories of my own grandmother, spending her last days in such a place after suffering a paralyzing stroke. My mood remained somber until we got to Sister Rose's room. It was decorated with construction paper flowers and children's drawings, with family photos and "Get Well" cards done in crayon covering a lamp table near her bed.

Sister Rose was loved by many.

Propped up in a hospital bed, her emaciated legs uncovered, I could see her frailty. White hair, light brown skin, thin face (hardly wrinkled), partially covered by thick glasses obscuring a spark of awareness. Michael began the conversation.

"Hi, I'm Pastor Mike and this is my friend Phil." Coming close to shake her hand, "Pastor Santana said we could come and meet you."

Sister Rose turned to get Santana's approval, sitting in a chair on her left. He nodded, and as Michael let her right hand go, she took Santana's left hand in hers.

Michael's enthusiasm was evident as he gently sought to confirm the story.

Sister Rose spoke little, and only after checking with Santana. When Michael finished, the room went silent as Sister Rose chose not to respond.

It was my turn to press in. "Please, Sister Rose, tell me, did you forgive Santana of this terrible crime?"

"Mijo," she responded, looking to Santana.

"Yes, it's okay, Sister, they can be trusted."

"Santana was a very bad boy, but that is not who he is now." With that, she nodded her head up and down for emphasis, before squeezing Santana's hand and turning toward him, away from me. Our conversation was over.

I had my answer, and remarkable as it might be, I was sure it was true.

I would never doubt the power of forgiveness again.

CHAPTER TWO

Saving Sergeant Tahmooressi

S ergeant Andrew Tahmooressi served two tours with the Marine Corps in Afghanistan before being placed on inactive status and returning home. In March of 2014, he drove from his home in Florida to the Veteran's Hospital in San Diego, California, to receive treatment for a Traumatic Brain Injury (TBI) and Post-Traumatic Stress Disorder (PTSD) as a result of an improvised explosive device (IED) that threw him from his position atop a Humvee as a .50 machine gun operator. His performance in combat included an engagement for which he was given a rare promotion on the battlefield to Sergeant for valor and gallantry.

On March 31, 2014, Andrew, with all of his worldly possessions in his truck, including three firearms legal to possess in the state of Florida, mistakenly exited the last off-ramp on Interstate Highway 5 going south into Mexico at the Tijuana border. He attempted to turn around before leaving the United States. Unable to do so before reaching the border, he asked a Mexican federal officer if he could simply go back into the United States. Instead, he was sent to secondary inspection where, when asked about what was in his truck. He freely told them about the guns and where they were located. Bringing firearms into Mexico is a serious offense for which he could receive a sentence of twenty-one years in prison.

I was asked by Jill Tahmooressi, Andrew's mother, to collect evidence on this side of the border and assist in the selection of legal counsel in Mexico. The Mexican legal process took over 210 days, during which time Andrew was held in custody in two different Mexican prisons. As time passed, frustration in the United States over his continued confinement grew into a media firestorm, and a political movement calling for sanctions against Mexico. This effort was supported by a variety of political pundits, celebrities, and politicians, the most prominent of whom were Oliver North of Freedom Alliance and future presidential candidate Donald Trump. Anger festered on both sides of the border as the continued imprisonment of an American war hero served the purposes of anti-Mexico politicians in the United States, and nationalist sentiments in Mexico stoked by the perceived interference in their criminal justice system and resentment over the thousands of Mexican citizens imprisoned in the United States.

The following story is but one example of the courage and effort it took to win Andrew's release. A relentless battle fought on both sides of the border by Andrew's mother, myself, my investigator, Len Newcomb, and a courageous Mexican lawyer, Fernando Benitez.

《《 》》

I was nervous the first time I met Jill, but she put me at ease immediately. Picking her up at the airport in San Diego prior to our trip to Tijuana Federal Court, I was immediately struck by her calm demeanor and obvious resolve. A successful professional in her own right, she researched my background and quickly thanked me for signing on.

Andrew had already been incarcerated for three months, and Jill's battle to win his freedom was in full swing. My commitment was not only based upon my belief in his innocence, but also my distress at learning he was an inmate at La Mesa Prison.

Having regularly traveled to the suburbs of Tijuana over the previous twenty-five years to build houses for the poor with Baja Christian Ministries (BCM), I was familiar with the Baja Peninsula and its people. My work with BCM and Prison Fellowship (PF) took me into La Mesa and Ensenada prisons. La Mesa was the most desperate place I had ever been. A 16' x 20' cell held as many as twenty men. Some of them were three to a bunk. Basic necessities of life, such as food, soap, toothpaste, and toilet paper were not provided by the prison. Relief organizations like BCM and PF regularly went into La Mesa to distribute these supplies.

I also knew La Mesa to be notorious for the control cartel members have over the other inmates. Their influence extends beyond prison walls into urban neighborhoods in both Mexico and the United States. One inmate of La Mesa was known to be in charge of organizing the entire drug trade in

Ventura County, California, where I did most of my criminal defense practice.

BCM and PF were critical to Andrew's survival as he received regular spiritual counseling from Pastor Luis Benitez Juarez. It is no exaggeration to suggest Pastor Luis's care and compassion may have saved Andrew's life. Andrew's level of despair, combined with his PTSD, left him so despondent as to consider suicide as his only escape from the nightmare he was living.

When first incarcerated at La Mesa Prison, Andrew was surrounded by other prisoners and told they were "hit men" in a drug cartel. They sought to extort protection money from Andrew and his family. It started like this, "The only way you are going to get out of here is on a stretcher, dead." This didn't work on the hardened Marine, so they went to threats of gang rape. Finally, when they told Andrew they could find out where his family lived and have his mother murdered, his PTSD kicked in. "Improvise, adapt, and overcome"—this Marine Corps motto took charge of Andrew's mind. Andrew decided he should escape La Mesa.

His plan was impulsive in design, but extraordinary in execution. As the prison guards later reported, "he scaled the fence like a Ninja," got to the top, cleared the razor wire, and dropped down to the other side. A rifle shot echoed off the prison walls, but Andrew was undeterred. Having made it over the main fence, he sprinted for the exterior chain-link fences that surrounded the perimeter of the prison. He scaled the first with ease throwing himself over and landing on his feet. One fence to go, but the guards were on him. As he reached the top of the second fence, he felt someone grab his foot, but he managed to pull away and again throw himself over the razor wire. When he landed, a squad of guards surrounded him. Thrown to the ground, Andrew prepared himself for the promised beating.

Clubbed in the back, kicked in the ribs, forced to his knees; then repeatedly slapped back and forth across the face. Blood flowed freely from his lips and nose, but Andrew resolved himself to endure it like a Marine captured by the enemy. In fact, as he later reported, "I was grateful that my punishment left no permanent injury."

Placed in handcuffs and hog-tied, they carried him like a side of beef on a pole back to the prison. There he was held spread eagle by restraints to the four posts of a bunk in an isolation cell. Andrew remained tortured like this for two weeks.

Isolation can be the cruelest punishment, particularly for someone suffering from PTSD. Finally allowed to move about in his cell; in a moment of despair Andrew took the only chance he had to escape his torment.

Jill received a phone call from William Whitaker, unit chief of the United States Consulates Office in Tijuana, Mexico. "Mrs. Tahmooressi, Andrew tried to kill himself. He is okay, though he was found in a pool of blood. He broke a light bulb and cut his neck, but he's going to live. He's in the prison infirmary now under constant surveillance."

Jill took in this revelation like the professional she is, but soon left her office for the privacy of her car. Clutching the steering wheel, the tears she held back for so long began to flow. Next came the gut-wrenching wails of a wounded animal in agony. As she emptied herself of grief, a new emotion took root in her consciousness, a sense that she was not alone.

"As the pain poured out, peace flowed in. A blanket of warmth surrounded me; it surpassed all understanding." Jill cried out to God in prayer. A mother's prayer for the life of her only son.

Jill's paralyzing fear now faced new courage. No longer would she live in terror of the next horror she heard about Andrew. A resolve to take action set in; no more sitting idle and hoping for the best. She would find a way to save him.

The next day Jill received a phone call from Andrew. Pressure from the consulates' office and concern about negative publicity in the U.S. made it happen. Before long the inevitable question: "Were you really trying to kill yourself?"

"Yes," was his only reply. Jill made no further inquiry, rather she broke into prayer. Andrew later reported, "My mom prayed over me and it gave me the strength to escape out of that life-threatening situation." Andrew had hope—hope he would survive, and he might even be set free someday.

Jill reasoned her best strategy involved the news media and politicians. Andrew's background and current circumstances made for a compelling story and worthy cause. She started with Congresswoman Debbie Wasserman-Schultz, Jill's representative in Florida and a few local media outlets. The story of an Afghanistan war hero wrongfully held in a Mexican prison got picked up across the nation. Fox News covered it daily. Various Fox commentators, and Greta Van Susteren in particular, championed Andrew's release. The publicity and political influence caused Andrew's transfer to El Hongo Prison in Tecate. A modern maximum-security facility, Andrew wouldn't get another chance to escape, but they could keep him away from the other inmates. He was still in prison, but for the time being he was safe.

≪ ≪ ≫ ≫

El Hongo Prison rises out of the Mexican desert like a monument to despair. It is a modern megalopolis surrounded by an exterior concrete gray wall, some fifteen feet tall, further enclosed by a chain-link fence with razor wire at the top. The area between is designed to create a kill zone visible to the towers strategically distanced apart, so the marksmen have a clear shot at any inmate caught within.

At El Hongo, Andrew's mental and spiritual health improved as he received regular visits from local missionaries. Andrew grew bolder in his faith, even to the point of walking around the prison yard with Pastor Luis singing "Onward Christian Soldiers."

We journeyed into Mexico to get a briefing from Andrew's current lawyer and state department officials at the American consulate in Tijuana. This time we were accompanied by Efren Cortez. Efren worked for an international security company whose CEO had been following Andrew's story in the press. Concerned for Jill's safety while in Mexico, the CEO offered to have Efren act as our driver, interpreter, and security officer. Efren served in Afghanistan and Iraq as an Army Ranger. A veteran of 500 combat missions, Efren was capable, competent, and fearless. His mere presence gave us courage.

The meeting at the consulate didn't go well. It soon became apparent Andrew's lawyer was in way over his head: "He never crossed into Mexico; he was in the neutral zone when he was stopped." I noticed Mr. Whitaker cringe at this assertion. I then asked, "Is there such a thing as a neutral zone?" Whitaker quickly answered, "No, there is not." He then followed me into the men's room for an off-the-record conversation. There I was told our lawyer never read the court file, and he already missed a crucial deadline for filing a motion to dismiss.

When we got back to the car, I explained this to Jill, and she quickly accepted my recommendation to get a new lawyer. We went back into the consulate to ask for a recommendation. The first guy we called thought it too hot to handle: "I don't do political cases." The second, Fernando Benitez, already knew the case, and agreed to see us that day.

Fernando Benitez was the real deal. He had all the outward trappings of success—large, dark wood-paneled conference room in his downtown Tijuana office, and a small army of junior lawyers and assistants—he obviously knew what it took to win. In his mid-forties, Fernando stood just under six feet, with dark well-trimmed and slightly graying hair and matching beard. Speaking impeccable English, he could not have been more presentable. But what impressed me most about Fernando was his willingness to listen. Jill and I had countless questions which Fernando patiently answered in detail. His enthusiasm for Andrew's case was obvious, and his courage undeniable. Jill soon made the decision—which would later prove pivotal—to hire Fernando Benitez. He would see Andrew's case to its conclusion.

The consulate made arrangements for Jill to visit Andrew at El Hongo. Efren and I followed the State Department Suburban carrying Jill and other consulate staff. When we arrived, we were told only Jill would be allowed in and she would have to endure a strip search before entering. Efren and I were outraged. It seemed to me nothing less than an intimidation tactic. Jill was resolute, telling us, "Not to worry, I'm a nurse, I'm used to bodily inspections." Still, Efren and I seethed at the thought of this beautiful lady having to endure such an indignity to visit her son. Perhaps it was best we waited outside.

As it turned out we would not be alone. There were two lean-to shacks, one on each side of the road. One functioned as a small store, set up just next to a drainage pipe from the prison spewing raw sewage onto the desert floor. The second, as a sort of bus stop, where four men and a woman sat waiting for something. We parked near the bus stop, and I thought we might walk around the perimeter of the prison to get a better look at it. We didn't get far before two guards with M-16s approached us, concerned we might be casing the joint. We returned to the car to wait however long it took for Jill to return. The crew at the bus stop gave us the once-over as we passed.

They could have been cast in *The Good, the Bad and the Ugly*, as all of the men had the hardened look of the recently incarcerated. One man—the youngest and strongest—was of particular concern. As we walked by, I noticed he held a seven-iron in his right hand and was rhythmically slapping it into his left. As we reached the car the woman called to us, "Why are you here?"

I took the bait, explaining who we were there to see. She knew Andrew's story, and that he was at El Hongo, so I didn't have to give details.

"I've been coming to this prison for twenty years to visit my son." I heard Efren rustling around behind me, I had violated his rules of engagement.

"See those vans over there? I take some of the men home, let 'em stay with me if they have nowhere to go."

"That's gotta be a lot of men, over twenty years."

"Not really, they don't let too many out, maximum security and all. When I get a new one, I drop someone off in Tijuana, I try to get 'em on their feet."

Impressed, but thinking of Efren, I just nodded.

"Look at this guy, he just did ten years, no family, no clothes, got nothin.'"

I noticed the tall, thin man in the middle dressed in gray—gray T-shirt, gray sweat pants, and shoes that could no longer be held together by the tape applied some time ago.

"The problem," she continued, "even if he got to Tijuana, everyone knows he's a convict—he won't have a chance."

About my height, thinner—I opened the trunk and grabbed my suitcase. "Three shirts, two pairs of pants, assorted socks and underwear, that should do him for a while." I thought better of it for a moment, then took forty bucks from my wallet and slipped it into the pant pocket. Efren was on me at the car, but instead of a scolding, he pulled out a new shirt of his own. "Might as well be all in," he muttered.

"Here, have him try these on."

She stood and ran to us, dust-stained tears ran down her cheeks. "Bless you both, this will make all the difference."

The man in gray remained seated, until she returned to him saying, "*Para ti, la ropa es para ti.*" He disappeared out the back, clothes in hand. The other two men got up and moved toward us. I feared a shakedown, until the older one extended his hand, *"Muchas gracias, señor."*

"De nada," was all the Spanish I knew.

Our moment didn't last as the black Suburban pulled up returning Jill. It had gone well; she lifted Andrew's spirits with hope of a winning strategy. They even chose to forgo the strip search. All Jill wanted to do now was go home.

Efren took charge, directing us to the car, fulfilling his part of the mission. As we pulled away, I saw the man in gray wearing Efren's shirt, my pants, and a delirious smile.

≪ ≪ ≫ ≫

The criminal justice system of Mexico is completely foreign to any practitioner of the common law tradition in English-speaking countries. It is best characterized by a lack of transparency and the unequal treatment afforded prosecution and defense. The defendant actually appears guilty until proven innocent. The prosecution is brought by the "Public Ministry," which is also responsible for investigating the charge. It is endowed with "public faith," such that its actions are almost incontrovertible. Historically, there has been no right to cross-examination. Guilt or innocence, and the appropriate sentence, is determined by a single judge in a document entitled "Final Resolution." A lack of procedural time limits, or sanctions for failing to timely submit a case, allows defendants to be held in custody for years without a finding of guilt or innocence. For a criminal defense lawyer used to public trials requiring live witnesses, cross-examination, and—best of all— twelve impartial jurors, Mexican criminal procedure was a nightmare I could hardly fathom.

Fernando took great pains to explain it to me when we were alone, knowing my reaction would not instill confidence in Jill. Fortunately, Mexico passed a judicial reform law in 2008 adopting many of the procedural safeguards of an adversarial system. The reform was to be gradually implemented, and our judge had already granted Fernando the opportunity to question the border agents.

The hearing took place in a federal courthouse in Tijuana. We were there to observe the agents' testimonies and submit video evidence of the freeway entrance and border vortex on Interstate 5. The video was prepared by my long-time private investigator Len Newcomb. Len also took pictures of the freeway entrance sign that was so covered in graffiti the "SOUTH" portion was nearly impossible to read.

Unintentional entry into Mexico was a defense to the charges, but the burden of proving it was on us. Getting the video into evidence was not a sure thing under the rules of procedure developed before the advent of the electronic age.

Efren drove us again and took care of all the logistics. He was particularly good with the locals since he was born in Mexico and regularly visited family on the Baja Peninsula.

When we arrived at the courthouse in Tijuana, we were surprised by the throng of reporters waiting outside. The case had become big news on both sides of the border. Fox News provided coverage nightly as Mexico's continued imprisonment of an American war hero drew huge Nielsen ratings. Conservative politicians also jumped on the band-wagon calling out the Mexican government and blaming the Obama Administration for failing to win Andrew's release. This created a political backlash in Mexico among nationalist politicians and media who felt bullied by the United States. They claimed hypocrisy, since the United States was detaining thousands of their citizens caught trying to cross the border. Getting Jill safely through this gauntlet and into the courthouse was our first concern.

We decided to park down the street at Fernando's office and walk over. Efren at point, Len—another sizeable man— was behind, with Fernando and me covering Jill's flanks as we made our way down the broken sidewalk. The exterior of the courthouse was protected by a slated steel fence, and no press was allowed within its perimeter. Walking proved a strategic advantage, as the media thought we would arrive in vehicles on the street. We managed to slip in a side gate with few of them noticing. Once inside they surrounded the fence pleading with Jill for a quote before she went in. It didn't happen.

Len and Efren were denied entry. Jill and I got in, but we weren't allowed in the "courtroom." I use this term loosely as nothing about it reminded me of a space where justice is honored. Rather, it was a cramped little office with white-washed walls except for the one containing a cage where Andrew was kept. The steel mesh had an opening about five feet off the floor through which Andrew could observe the hearing, but he had to stand the entire time. The interior of the building was under construction, the ceiling had no tiles, and ancient insulation dropped asbestos at regular intervals. The hallway had no benches, only a couple of broken chairs, which we quickly commandeered. Only the judge, the attorneys, Michael Veassy of the American Consulate, and a witness could fit in the room when court was in session.

Jill and I spent many long hours together waiting for any news of what was going on inside. At various breaks in the proceedings, Fernando and Mr. Veassy briefed us—Veassy recounting the testimony and Fernando explaining the significance.

As evening approached, I stepped outside to get some fresh air. Seeing me, the assembled media cried out for any scrap of information. I had nothing to tell them, but they had some news for me.

"Your security guy got arrested."

Efren? Oh no . . .

"What are you saying?" I thought it a ploy until a Mexican reporter provided details. "Yah, I saw it go down. They were looking for the big guy, and when your security guy told 'em he left in a taxi, they arrested him."

Not good, I thought, *we're already down one, don't want to lose another*. I scanned the crowd for Len, who was nowhere to be found.

I went back inside to let Jill and Fernando know what was going on. The trial had adjourned for the day. We braved the gauntlet of reporters and walked back to Fernando's office.

Once inside, Denise, a paralegal with the office, led us upstairs, stopping in front of a corner shelf filled with leatherbound books. Denise reached behind the bookcase, then put her shoulder to one side. Slowly the bookcase rotated out revealing a classically appointed wet bar and lounge within. Len, sitting alone at a booth, wine glass half full, looked as miserable as I've ever seen him.

"Phil, I didn't do anything!"

"I'm just glad to see you; Debbie would have never forgiven me if I left you behind. What happened?"

"Nothing happened! Efren and I decided to get some lunch, and this little Latina sits down with us, says she's a reporter with the Zeta paper."

"I'm sure that didn't work on you guys, being on the job and all—she didn't buy you any drinks, did she?"

"We didn't tell her anything, so she got frustrated after a while, which was kind of fun . . ." I smiled, picturing them enjoying the moment.

"So, she gets mad and leaves, we pay the bill and walk back to the courthouse, then we see her talking to some Federales. Efren gets it before I do, so he tells me to get back to Fernando's office ASAP."

"Good advice, you took it of course."

"I protested a little, but he convinced me, you know the whole language thing and all."

"Anyway, he comes back to the office and tells me that chick said I put my hand on her leg; that's a lie, Phil."

"I know, Len. So, where's Efren?"

"He said the cops were going to see if she wanted to press charges, since it was me they were after. Fernando left me in this safe room and Efren went outside to see if they'd come back."

Denise, who'd been listening with Jill at the bar, walked over to tell us, "They pushed Efren hard on where you were, I heard him say he put you in a taxi headed for the border. Next thing I know they're arresting him."

Jill made her way over to the booth and sat next to Len, "It'll be alright; we'll get him out, right, Denise?"

"Of course, I'm sure Mr. Benitez is working on it as we speak, I'll check with him."

"I'm coming with you," I said as I followed Denise back through the bookcase.

Fernando was on the phone, doing all the talking in Spanish. He signaled for us to sit down, and Denise to interpret, "He's talking to one of our . . . what do you say? Ah, 'people' who make the rounds for us at night. We're trying to get bail for him, you know the fine amount."

I really didn't know, but it sounded good.

Fernando hung up with "gracias" and turned to me. "I got a hold of the bailiff, he's a friend of mine, and he thinks $300 ought to do it. We got somebody going there now."

"You got courts open this time of night?"

"Sure, I know a bail officer . . . just got to know how to get a hold of her."

Fernando's lips creased enough of a smile for me to appreciate the skill level of my Mexican colleague. Extra-judicial methodology is a talent I admire.

"Since this is one of my people, at least let me pay the fine," I insisted. "After all, they let themselves get set up for this."

"No, no, can't do that, there's more to this than you know. The same reporter has been trying to interview me. I kept putting her off; you know it's a political thing. I represented the mayor of Tijuana on gun charges—he had over a thousand firearms and 10,000 rounds of ammunition at his hacienda, and you're only allowed three. I eventually walked him on a search warrant issue. Anyway, Zeta didn't like it. They think the mayor's business partner murdered their founder, they got a grudge. So, they were coming after me—you know, my people—anyway they could."

"Wow," I replied. "That's putting yourself out there, isn't it?"

"I don't know, I just did my job, they're making it personal. It's the cost of doing business here." Fernando shrugged, like no big deal.

"Zeta's left wing, they've been running editorials about Andrew's case. It's time to stand up to the bully to the north, that sort of thing."

I tried to process it all, but soon returned to more immediate concerns. "So, you're going to get Efren out tonight?"

"Sure, no problem, my connection is reliable. Efren should be out in an hour or so, but the trick is getting Len out of here. They'll be looking for him."

"I'm sure you got a plan, been here, done this before?"

"Yeah, well as you know every case is different, but we have our ways. Denise, why don't you take Len to the border. Have him lie down in the back and drop him off at the place to walk over. You can drive, Jill; they'll probably be watching your car, you know."

"I get it, we're the decoy, but what about Efren?"

"That pastor guy," Fernando looked to Denise, "Luis?"

"Right, he said he'd do anything to help, I'll give him a call." Denise rose to leave the office.

"She's going to be a lawyer soon, I recommended her for the Bar, that's how you get licensed here."

"She'd be a sure thing over the border. Women are about half the law school grads these days."

"Really, we got a ways to go, it's still a man's world here. A lot of judges don't take women lawyers seriously."

Fernando and I spent another ten minutes chit-chatting, trying to play it cool until the phone rang. Fernando answered mid-ring. More Spanish, but Fernando winked so I knew it was good news.

I later learned Efren spent more than six hours in a cell with twenty other prisoners, handcuffed to the bars so he looked like he was about to be flogged. All the other prisoners were free to move about. Needless to say, he felt quite vulnerable. The local police continued to question him about Len's whereabouts, but he never wavered, his story didn't change.

When brought before a judge, Efren noticed his accuser was there to make her accusation stick. She told an elaborate story about how both he and Len ran their hands down her leg while they were sitting across from her at lunch. The totality of her lies was more than Efren could bear. As a Ranger, Efren could keep his wits about him in the face of danger. This was a different threat, however, in a foreign arena he did not understand. It was hard not to fear he would end up like Andrew, sitting in a Mexican prison with no end in sight.

When asked to speak, Efren began by declaring a traditional oath. "Upon the life of my infant son, I tell you what this woman is saying is a lie. Why, Your Honor, did she first accuse my friend, and only when she found out he was gone did she accuse me? She talked with us for hours, and never once did she complain about us to anyone."

Handcuffed behind his back, with the bailiff standing close by, Efren turned to face his accuser. "I can't believe you would lie about me like this. What we talked about was my family . . . how my wife and son are Mexican citizens, and how I grew up in Monterey. I showed you pictures of my family, my baby boy—and now you come here and denounce my good name, my sacred honor, and try to take me away from my family with your lies."

Efren's presentation was consistent with the righteous indignation of an innocent man. The judge was clearly moved, but with plenty of other cases to decide that night, she'd heard enough. Bail was set at three hundred dollars to be forfeited upon release.

Returning to the present, Fernando hung up telling me, "He'll be out in an hour, guess he actually got in front of a judge. The fine's been paid."

Denise returned to the chair next to me and announced, "Pastor Luis will be there in half an hour to pick him up and take him across the border. Where should we drop him off?"

"There's a Jack in the Box just on the other side right where the railroad tracks cross over." My border expertise finally came in handy. "Sounds like we got a plan, let's make it work."

We returned to the bar to find Jill at the table saying a prayer over Len. We waited an awkward moment for the "amen."

Fernando laid the plan out for them. Jill liked being the decoy; Len liked making a run for the border.

"We've got a back exit into an alley off the street. Phil, you walk out with Jill, and as soon as you get to the car, Denise will pull out in front and take you to the border."

"When we get to the ramp for the border crossing, I'll flash the high beams, you go up the ramp, and I'll continue on to the walk-across."

I nodded, indicating I would follow wherever she led.

Denise signaled for us to follow her to the back of the bar. There she pushed on the wall—sliding it sideways, she created an opening leading to a circular marble staircase twisting down into darkness.

"We call this the Harry Potter staircase," she quipped. I felt like I was following Emma Watson through Hogwarts. Reaching the top of the stairs, I hesitated. The white marble stairs barely reflected the light from above, and there were no handrails. I thought about waiting for someone to turn on a light, but hearing Denise's heels clicking down the steps, I was shamed into following her.

As my eyes adjusted, I could see we were in a parking garage. Denise opened the door to a VW Bug, moving the driver's seat forward saying to Len, "I think you can fit in there." Len squeezed himself into the back, his head just below the windows. Denise slapped the garage door opener and the night sky came into view. As Denise got in the Bug, Jill and I walked out looking for our rental.

All my senses were on high alert, looking for trouble at every turn. If they were staking us out, this was our most vulnerable moment. The street was vacant but for our car. We got in as Denise pulled out; starting up, we pulled in right behind her.

Following her through Tijuana traffic at night was a challenge. Finally, we approached the overpass filled with cars waiting to cross. Denise flashed her high beams and we broke away.

Pulling in, I had to swerve to the right to let a car backing down the overpass get past us. Unnerved, I recovered by remembering where I was, and how I'd seen many a maneuver like that on a Mexican highway. Safely up the ramp, we arrived at the back of the line. Experience told me about an hour to get to customs. We were on the slow road home.

Then, there they were. Two Federales walking along the overpass, flashlights inspecting every car in line. I looked at Jill—no sign of panic, stoic as always. As the Federales approached on either side, shining their light through the window, I could see a smile forming at the edges of Jill's lips. She wasn't just enduring the moment; rather she relished the prospect of a triumph over Mexican law enforcement.

Having inspected us in front, they turned their flashlights on the back seat, nothing there. No trunk in a SUV, they lingered, spoke in hushed tones, and moved on. We savored the moment in quiet gratitude as our thoughts turned to our friends, hoping they would fare as well.

The line moved better then I predicted; soon we were handing our passports to a U.S. Customs agent.

"What was the purpose of your visit to Mexico?"

"We had an appearance in Mexican federal court in Tijuana," I answered. He was looking at Jill's passport.

"Yes, I recognize the name. I hope it goes well for you."

"Thank you," Jill replied as he returned our passports.

"You know, just last week we had a Mexican police officer come through, we found two firearms with ammunition. We just let him turn around and go back to Mexico."

"Hardly seems fair, does it?" I said.

"No, it doesn't," he acknowledged. "Anyway, welcome to the United States, and please know how many of us are with you." This was the nicest conversation I'd ever had at the border.

Winding our way through the serpentine gauntlet of center dividers and speed bumps installed since 9/11, we finally arrived on Interstate 5 going north, we were home. Taking the first exit, we came to a stop across the street from Jack in the Box.

It was after one in the morning, but the intersection was bustling with people. The electric trains were still running, carrying people back and forth over the border, others walked over; many of whom carried luggage. The Jack in the Box was lit up and the parking lot was jammed. As we pulled in, we caught a break—someone leaving gave us a spot in front. Then I saw Len, all six-foot-three and two-hundred-eighty pounds of him, the tough old gumshoe even smiled at me. I jumped out, ran to my old friend, throwing my arms around him. Under normal circumstances I would have embarrassed him—not tonight. Back in the good old U.S. of A., Len was one happy patriot.

Len's passage was uneventful. "Denise dropped me off at the footbridge crossing. I had no trouble getting in line for customs. When I got there, they didn't like that I didn't have a passport, but when I showed them my retired Oxnard detective's badge, they let me right through. Sure is one great country, isn't it, Phil?"

I had to smile at that one. "You bet, Len. At times like these we appreciate it more than ever."

Only Efren was missing. He started for the border before Len, so he should have made it by now. I envisioned a triumphant reunion, yet we remained one man down. My cell service restored crossing the border, so I called him, but all I got was his recording. It occurred to me we might be in for a very long night. Having not eaten all day, even a Jumbo Jack looked good. I went inside to order. Then, I made the obligatory call to my wife, Rose. The rule had always been that upon crossing the border I would let her know I made it safely. I was very late, but she knew better than to worry about me.

I woke her. "Where have you been?"

"Well, it's a long story, and it's not over yet."

"I'm listening . . ." And so, I gave her as much as I could in the moment. I could imagine her shaking her head as she admonished me about my reckless friends and my own need to "flirt with danger."

"One of these days you're not going to get away with it, you know," she lovingly scolded me.

"But not today."

"Maybe for you, but your friend Efren is still not there, how long are you going to wait for him?"

"As long as it takes, my dear."

"Of course you are, and if he doesn't show up, you'll probably go back in looking for him, won't you?"

"Ahhhh, maybe, but that's not going to happen, he'll be here," I assured myself.

"Let Fernando handle it; you don't even speak the language."

"I guess you have a point there. I think he'll be here, not to worry."

"I gave that up long ago."

"Love you."

"Love you too."

Our conversation over, I sat down to a burger and fries. Quickly consumed, I headed outside to check on Jill. Then there he was . . . in a car driven by Pastor Luis. Efren smiled. No longer the soldier on duty, he jumped out to grab my hand, followed with a chest bump.

"Where have you been?"

"Luis didn't want to let go of me, so we drove across the border," Efren replied. "I was afraid you might've left by now," he said with relief.

"No, that wasn't going to happen."

Tears formed which I hoped could not be seen in the dark. Efren came in again, pounding my back with his powerful hands.

Efren was out, he was safe. We all made it out. Mission accomplished.

The four of us huddled in a circle. We didn't want to let go of one another. We ended with a prayer of gratitude for ourselves, and a new petition for the one we left behind.

« « » »

Andrew was coming up on four months of incarceration. As the legal proceedings dragged on, frustration turned into anger north of the border. All of the major news outlets were following the story, and Jill would often do multiple interviews in a day. Radio commentator Glenn Beck did a daily segment always ending with a count on the days he had been wrongfully imprisoned. Fox News commentators also called for his release and increasingly cast blame upon the Obama Administration for not pressuring, or even sanctioning, Mexico for his continued detention.

I confronted this position when I did an interview on Lou Dobbs's show not long after our return from Mexico. I was aware that Dobbs had strong anti-immigration views, but I truly believed the interview would be about the legal proceedings, and did not anticipate it would devolve into a demand I label the entire Mexican legal system as corrupt, or express outrage that President Obama, "as the Commander in Chief," had not yet called the president of Mexico demanding Andrew's release. Fernando counseled Jill and me about the danger of inflaming nationalist sentiments in Mexico, and the misguided perception that the United States could bully Mexico into releasing an American citizen without first adjudicating the case in a Mexican court.

Eventually, I was forced to explain, "I have a client in front of a judge in the Mexican judicial system, and that man is going to decide Andrew's fate, and I have to respect that, because that is how this case will be decided."

"What I care about is our audience getting the straight-up truth about the actions of our government that have utterly failed . . ." Needless to say, my interview with Lou Dobbs didn't end well. I wasn't about to say anything that might hurt Andrew's chances in court, and he wasn't about to let his audience down. When Lou Dobbs called to have me on the show again, I didn't return the call.

Jill faced far greater challenges regarding individuals and various interest groups seeking to exploit Andrew's circumstances for political or financial reasons. Various "influential" people in Mexico could "speak to the right people" and secure his release for an appropriate fee. Even "witches" claiming supernatural powers sought Jill out, which she particularly found offensive. Harder to discern were self-described passionate supporters of Andrew who wanted to raise money on his behalf, or organize a protest against Mexico. Jill, as always, held to a strict ethical standard consistent with her Christian beliefs. In a correspondence to one such group she told them:

> Please know I respect your impassioned support of my son Sergeant Andrew Tahmooressi. [But], comments that may be perceived by Mexican press as offensive to Mexico's dignity, and any inference that I either support those comments or the organization . . . could have a detrimental effect on our goal of having Andrew released as soon as possible . . . So, to reiterate, please do not associate me with any of your comments or activities . . . Peaceful, non-obstructive support is appreciated, yet I do not endorse any activity that collects money for events.

Of course, many fine people did offer their support in thoughtful and meaningful ways. "Free Sergeant Tahmooressi," signs appeared on billboards, T-shirts, and in small business windows throughout the nation. Jill rode in a "Free Andrew Tahmooressi" motorcycle rally on Independence Day in Florida, and more than 75,000 people followed daily updates posted on a Facebook page set up by volunteers. Over 100,000 people signed a petition on the White House website promising a response when that many signatures were obtained. Unfortunately, the Obama Administration took three months to respond, and the response was tepid at best. Diplomatic language such as ". . . our goal is to see that Mr. Tahmooressi is treated fairly," and Mexican authorities have been very willing to engage on this issue," only added to the perception the

Commander in Chief did not particularly care about a Marine who had most courageously served his country.

Various people of prominence, mostly politicians, and celebrities also offered their support. Freedom Alliance led by retired Lt. Col Oliver North made a donation of $10,000 to be used for legal fees, talk show host Montel Williams provided public relations services, and the former Energy Secretary in the Clinton administration and former New Mexico Governor Bill Richardson, assisted through his Center for Global Engagement. Congresswoman Debbie Wasserman Schultz, the Tahmooressis' local representative in Florida, was an early and consistent advocate for Andrew, and then later Congressmen Duncan Hunter and Ed Royce of California aggressively pushed the Obama Administration to take a stronger position. Ultimately, the Subcommittee for the Western Hemisphere chaired by Congressman Royce scheduled a hearing on the matter for October 1, 2014. Jill and I were hopeful Andrew would be released before the hearing.

On September 9, 2014, I once again escorted Jill to a scheduled hearing in Tijuana. Having already cross-examined the Mexican border guards, Fernando subpoenaed the video surveillance recordings to see if their testimony lined up with the video. It took months to get the recordings, as the Mexican border officials ignored the subpoena. Finally, the judge issued an arrest warrant for the custodian of records if the video was not provided.

On September 9, the judge, prosecutor, and Fernando spent more than twelve hours watching the video. Jill and I once again waited in the hallway to receive a report on the proceedings. It was after nine o'clock that evening before a tired, but delighted Fernando Benitez came to us and reported, "the video completely contradicts the version of the facts given by the border guards. I made a request to re-examine them, but the prosecutor said they had hired their own lawyers, who advised them not to testify again. This alone, may be enough for the judge to dismiss the case."

This was a special moment between Fernando and me, as it was apparent his skill and courage brought about this result. Fernando put himself personally at risk simply by taking on Andrew's case, and now he had taken down the Federales. I knew how it felt, the elation of proving a man's innocence by catching his accusers in a lie, but also the underlying prospect of retribution for embarrassing those in power.

It was not to be, however, despite the strength of our case in court. The judge took no immediate action. The Congressional hearing went ahead as scheduled, and Jill once again handled herself beautifully. Her opening statement was heart-wrenching as she went with a theme of "memorable quotes from my high-achieving son." These included, "God nudged me to join the military. I'll be enlisting in the Marines. We just got hit with an IED. I've been arrested [in Mexico] and I'm not going to make it through the night. There are hit men in the cell with me and they've told me they're going to kill me. Mom, I tried to kill myself because the guards and the inmates were going to rape, torture, and eventually execute me . . ." By the time she was finished, Jill owned everyone in the committee room. The remainder of the hearing was typical committee theater provided by members of Congress seeking political points. None of them came close to the sincere and thoughtful presentation Jill provided.

Not long after the hearing, I received a call from Fernando: "Phil, the judge has appointed a psychiatrist to confirm Andrew's PTSD diagnosis." I could tell Fernando was excited about this development, but I didn't get it.

"Fernando, the jails of the United States are filled with mental health patients, the largest mental health facility in the world is in the Los Angeles County Jail. So, what if he has PTSD, it's not a defense here. I've represented many a veteran with PTSD and it changes nothing for them."

"It's a defense in Mexico—we signed off on international human rights treaties that the United States refused to participate in. One of them calls for the humane treatment of inmates with a diagnosed mental illness, and our constitution requires us to provide treatment and rehabilitation for them."

"I still don't understand the relevance . . ."

"You see, we don't have veterans suffering from combat-related PTSD, so we have no protocols for treating the illness. If the psychiatrist confirms his PTSD, he will have to be released on human rights grounds, so he can receive treatment."

"Wow, the perfect diplomatic solution. No need to make a finding on guilt or innocence, just a grant of mercy, pointing out the benevolence of the Mexican criminal justice system."

"Exactly, I figure he should have a report in about a month."

"Good, because Jill tells me Andrew's not doing very well. He told her, 'I'm surrounded by evil in here,' things like that, similar to what he was saying when he attempted suicide. You should let the judge know this; it might speed up the process. A downward spiral in Andrew's mental health would not go over well north of the border. We've already got congressmen calling for sanctions and certain groups organizing boycotts and protests at the border."

"I know, things are getting hot here also. I'm getting my fair share of abuse; it gets old after a while." I knew Fernando was downplaying the level of stress he was under. Threats were made against him and, of course, he couldn't rely on law enforcement for protection. When we hung up the phone, I said a prayer for my newfound friend and his family.

Fernando and I decided it would be a good idea to leak out as much of the PTSD angle as possible. Letting the press know a resolution might be coming soon would calm tensions in the U.S. and prepare Mexico for Andrew's possible release. I called Dan Gallo of Fox News. Dan was the producer assigned to the Tahmooressi story. They were the first to pick it up, and the most supportive throughout. Due to their support, I promised Dan I would give him the scoop when we learned Andrew would be released.

So, I did an opinion piece for foxnews.com laying out the reasons I thought Andrew should be released concluding with:

> "I strongly believe that within the next four weeks U.S. Marine Sgt. Andrew Tahmooressi will be released from El Hongo Federal Prison in Mexico and able to walk on American soil again."

Fernando was sure Andrew would be released; he just didn't know when the order would come out. He traveled to San Diego to meet with Jill and me so he could brief us in person. Jill was staying in the Westgate Hotel, and when Bill

Richardson learned she was there, he had her room upgraded to the Presidential Suite.

We found out Fernando recently flew to Mexico City to meet with the Attorney General, ". . . and they are no longer opposing Andrew's release. They will be submitting the matter on the record and presenting no evidence in opposition. Once they formally file their non-opposition, the judge will make a final ruling."

I asked, "How long do you think that will take? If we were on this side of the border, he would be in court the next day, and the judge would just rule from the bench."

"I know, Phil, but we do everything in writing, so it has to be filed and ruled upon, the process is archaic, that's why we're changing it."

A strong knock from the door interrupted our conversation. I looked to Jill: "Are you expecting anyone?"

"No, not that I know of."

Fernando looked concerned, telling us, "We can't let any of this out yet, it could jeopardize everything if this hits the media before the judge officially makes a ruling."

"Alright, I'll answer the door and get rid of whoever it is, and you guys just keep talking."

As I headed for the door, I heard a stronger effort on the other side. I opened the door to see former New Mexico Governor Bill Richardson in coat and tie before me.

"I see Mr. Benitez is here, mind if I come in and participate in the briefing?"

"I'm sorry, this is a confidential attorney-client conversation, no one but the lawyers and Mrs. Tahmooressi can be in the room right now." Richardson was obviously not a man used to being told no. He proceeded to give the "Do you know who I am speech," and a description of his current involvement in the matter. He stepped forward expecting me to yield, I did not.

"I'm really sorry, sir, but I can't let you in, perhaps you can come back in half an hour, and we will tell you what we can at that time."

Richardson was hot, but he knew better than to press the issue. Eventually, he backed away and told me he'd come back in half an hour with the "rest of the team."

Returning, Jill asked, "Who was that?"

"Bill Richardson, he's not very happy with me right now, I wouldn't let him in."

Jill and Fernando chuckled at the that, with Fernando adding, "That's the way it's got to be, we don't need any politicians screwing this up right now."

"I told him to come back in half an hour, and you would brief him and 'his team,' then."

A half hour passed quickly as we discuss how much we could tell them. Fernando was reticent about telling them much of anything, but Jill pointed out, "Governor Richardson is providing a private plane to take us back to Florida, he needs to know when to have it ready. The plan is to fly us out of Brown Airfield just over the Otay Mesa border crossing."

"It seems to me, Fernando, we believe his release is imminent, but it could be a few more days. If we tell them that, they'll be ready for anything."

"My concern is if they tell that to the press, and it gets out in Mexico, we'll have a big backlash. They might even protest at the border, block off the streets. For his own security, we need to keep a lid on this. The other thing is, who's going to pick him up at El Hongo?"

"Mr. Veassy said they can help with that; they'll pick him up and take him over the border. I trust him, he's been nothing but attentive and professional." Jill never ceased to impress me, despite the excitement of this long-hoped-for moment, she still made decisions with the acumen of a health care professional looking out for a patient.

"Okay, so Fernando you do the talking, tell them as little as you think they need to know, without any of the details as to how you got it done."

Fernando smiled and nodded "yes," just as there was another knock at the door.

Quite a crew were assembled outside; I shook hands with each of them at the door. Governor Richardson with two assistants—Juan Massey and a young lady who only introduced herself as Mary—Jonathan Franks who described himself as a publicist, and Congressmen Matt Salmon and Ed Royce.

Fernando was masterful in his presentation. He's an expert at continuing to speak while saying very little if anything, new. When the questions come, he politely pled ignorance, and restated our official position. "It could be any day now, it's entirely within the judge's discretion. Anymore external pressure or press about what he is going to do, or should do, only jeopardizes the outcome." He concluded with an admonition, "It is critically important that no one tip the press off until Andrew is safely over the border. Just like your country we have certain nationalist sentiments that will not like this outcome, if given enough time to organize, they may show up at the border. Andrew's safe return must be our top priority."

Everyone present agreed, "Nothing is more important than bringing Andrew home safely."

A sense of unity of purpose touched everyone present. I was compelled to do something I don't think I've ever done before: say a prayer in a secular setting with people I don't even know. We were seated in a circle, so I asked, "I'd like to say a prayer, perhaps if we just stand, maybe hold hands . . . and I'll lead us." Not everyone was comfortable with my request, but I saw Jill was delighted. Just as we got to our feet and clasped hands with the people on either side of us, Mary fell to her knees. I was moved, to say the least.

"Dear Lord, we say a prayer for Andrew . . . it has been a long and difficult struggle, but You have allowed us to see the victory before us. Lord, we pray You keep Andrew safe. He has suffered too much, Lord, let him suffer no more. And we pray for our judge, that he be a good, decent, and caring man intent on doing justice. May he rightly discern the law and release Andrew to his family, friends, and his country. We ask all this in Jesus's name, amen."

The next day Jill and I went to a Padres game, their stadium was almost next door to the hotel. It was a typically beautiful day, like most in San Diego, but our attention was somewhere other than the game. It was like waiting for a jury verdict—you've done the best you can, you know there's going to be a resolution of some sort soon, but you don't know when it will be, and you can't do anything else to influence it.

After the game, I let Jill know I would be returning to my office in Ventura County. I had other clients, work was piling up, and it made no difference if I was there or not. If I got enough advance notice, I might try and make the drive to Brown Airfield for the celebratory moment, but I knew that was unlikely. My satisfaction would come from Fernando, who when he left San Diego told me, "Phil, you'll be my first call."

I spoke to Fernando several times over the next few days. That's what lawyers under stress do—we engage in speculation as to why it's taking so long, and what it is the judge must be doing. Then I got the call: "He'll be released today, in about two hours. I've got a copy of the order. He did go with the humanitarian grounds, but he also laid out facts the way we presented them. The prosecution had no objection to the dismissal of the charges—his case is dismissed."

"That's known as total victory, Fernando! Well done, my brother, well done."

"It'll probably take about three hours to get him to the border. It's two o'clock now, so let's say you can start letting the press know, about five o'clock."

"Got it, will do."

The second I got off the phone with Fernando, I let out a victory yelp, startling everyone in the office who never heard from me before. I was as excited about the result as I had ever been, hard fought and hard won. I thought of making the drive to Brown's Airfield, but with L.A. traffic there was no way I'd get there in time. So, I just sat back in my chair, savored the moment, and said a little prayer of thanks.

The moment was soon interrupted by my cell phone, the display read Dan Gallo, Fox News. I hesitated, I so much want to tell him, they deserve to know first, but I'd made a commitment.

"Hi, Dan, what's going on?"

"You tell me, Phil. AP just reported the judge has dismissed the case and ordered his release. They have a whole article up on it. Governor Richardson, of the Richardson Center, will be holding a press conference on his release at Brown Airfield in a couple hours, then flying by private jet home to Florida."

It's called "chumping," when some naïve newcomer is taken advantage of by the veterans of the street. In a word, I knew I'd been "chumped."

"Ahhh, I can neither confirm or deny that report, Dan, we had an understanding..."

"That's right, Phil, we did, you promised we'd get it first ..."

"Sorry, Dan."

"I gotta go follow up on an AP story."

The phone went silent, my joy in the moment diminished by the treachery of allies, and my own naivete.

My next move was to call Fernando, who was as surprised and disappointed as me to hear about the AP story. Fortunately, it took a while for it to get picked up in Mexico, so Andrew made it over the border without incident.

I later saw photographs of Andrew and Jill at Brown Airfield, along with Governor Richardson, Montel Williams, Jonathan Franks, and Representatives Royce and Salmon. All of the stories about Andrew's release gave the impression it was the result of some diplomatic coup orchestrated by celebrities and politicians. Nothing could be farther from the truth. Andrew's dismissal of all the charges that could have landed him in a Mexican prison for twenty-one years, was hard fought and won in a courtroom before a Mexican judge who considered all of the evidence.

The cross-examination of the border officials, and their subsequent impeachment by the border video, was so severe as to cause them to refuse to provide further testimony is what won the day. Andrew never intended to enter Mexico with firearms in his possession, his entry was a mistake, largely the fault of poor freeway signage, and he attempted to turn around when he got to the border. The truth matters, but it takes great skill and courage to present it in court, particularly in Mexico, based on everything I observed.

There is no doubt the media firestorm and political posturing created pressure on the Mexican government to release Andrew, but in the same vein it caused internal pressure not to release him. Resentment over treatment of Mexican nationals in U.S. custody inflamed nationalist sentiments passionately opposed to his release. We experienced the depths of that resentment during our fortuitous and skillful escape from Mexico in the middle of the night.

Despite all those who sought to take some credit for "bringing our Marine home," there are only two people who deserve it. The first is Fernando Benitez, who with great skill and compassion, successfully defended an innocent man, and did so at substantial personal risk to himself and his family. The second, and most significant is Jill Tahmooressi, who put her life on hold for seven months and did whatever it took to rescue her son. She did so with amazing strength and dedication, but more than that, she called upon the Holy Spirit in every decision she made. In times of peril, there is no greater wisdom than that which comes to us from heaven above.

CHAPTER THREE

The Candlesticks

Lillian, my administrative assistant, was out so I was answering my own phone. On such days I never got anything done—I listened to every train wreck calling in. This call was typical. Her older brother was in jail on two counts of robbery and he had a couple prior prison terms, which meant strike priors. Probably looking at twenty-five to life at a minimum. She was calling for her mother, who only spoke Spanish, so I had to wait for the translation on both ends.

"I know you don't want to go with the public defender, but some of them are very good and they are appointed to represent people who cannot afford a lawyer on cases just like this." I was pleading now, even though I knew it was lost in translation.

"My mother wants to know if we can come and see you today."

Oh boy, here we go again, why can't I just say no. "Ahhhh, I have other appointments this afternoon . . ."

"Okay, we'll come now, then."

They arrived at 10:30 a.m., a half hour early for their eleven o'clock. Well dressed, overly polite, and appreciative, I took them into my office right away. Mrs. Ramirez stood all of five feet with white hair making her look older than she was. Her daughter, Cecilia, was perhaps twenty. Bright and respectful, she patiently repeated my words in Spanish, listened to the response, and then spoke for her mother in perfect English. Clenched in Mrs. Ramirez's fist was a copy of my advertisement torn from the phone book.

I heard the facts as best as they knew them: "Rico has been a bad boy, but he has a good heart." Heard that one before. "He was doing good, graduated from the Victory Outreach men's home, until he backslid."

Now they had my attention. Over the years I represented dozens of men who were saved from prison and ordered to do a hard year at the men's home. My first backslider almost put me over the edge, knowing he would become the poster child for why programs don't work.

Bobby Frescas was a heroin addict, and his first stay at the men's home didn't stick. When I saw him in court again, I almost threw him against the wall; Pastor Bob had to restrain me. "Phil, we planted a seed, he's back for cultivation. It only has to work once."

Pastor Bob was right. Bobby Frescas made it the second time. Ten years clean and sober, government job, married with four beautiful kids, working as a traveling evangelist on the Victory Outreach circuit, paying it forward.

« « » »

The facts were miserable. Rico Ramirez, with a shaved head, prison tattoos on his bulging neck and arms, got really drunk and walked into a shoe store at the Oxnard Promenade. At first the two young ladies working the counter ignored him. He kept slurring his demand for all the money in the cash drawer, but they had seen ugly drunks before. Not until he got loud and angry did one of them slip downstairs and call mall security. Finally, alone and getting nervous, the remaining clerk opened the drawer, took out sixty bucks, and handed it to him.

Rico tried to stash the three twenties in his back pocket but didn't quite make it. Stumbling out, he barely made it to a planter where, as he sat down, the money fell out of his pocket onto the flowers below. He stayed there dazed and confused just long enough for the Oxnard P.D. to show up. Hooked up, twenties seized as evidence, victims interviewed enough to establish they gave him the money due to "force or fear," Rico was booked on two counts of robbery.

With his prison priors added to his three strike priors, I revised my earlier assessment to figure he was looking at thirty-three to life.

I didn't want this case—nowhere to go with it, no money.

"My mother wants you to know something, Mr. Dunn. She says she was praying over the phone book and God led her to your ad."

What could I say to that?

"She is just asking that you go see him, visit him in jail, then you will know what to do." Her dark brown eyes remained fixed upon my blue ones; she would not let me go until I agreed to her request. I was at her mercy.

"I'll go see him, but I'm not making any promises. I won't take his case unless I believe I can help somehow. Forgive me, but it looks pretty hopeless. They probably won't offer him anything—'plead and apply' they call it, or go to trial and get hammered. That's just the way it is."

As the translation goes through, I saw a smile come across her weathered lips, she leaned forward and stretched her hand across my desk to take mine in hers. "Thank you, sir," she told me, squeezing my palm with the strength only a career laborer has. I was hers now and she was mine—further resistance was futile.

Rico was short, perhaps 5'6", as he walked through the steel door on the other side of the visiting glass in the Ventura County Jail. He had spent eighteen of his forty-two years behind bars. He walked slowly with a little bounce in his step, reflecting the cocky attitude of the con wise. His hair had started to grow out, covering some of his tattoos, but his arms and neck were covered in ink, some of which I recognized as crudely done in prison. No artistry, but mucho respect on the street; Rico had been slammed down with the big homies.

A strong man, broad shouldered and heavily muscled from countless hours of working out in the yard, his first impression was menacing. Then he speaks.

"Mr. Dunn, thank you for coming." His tone was apologetic; I searched for signs of insincerity but found none.

"My mother said you would be coming. I really appreciate it, your being here. I heard about you when I was at the men's home. Those guys you represented love you."

A little embarrassed, I tried to get down to business. I went over the facts in the police reports. Rico didn't dispute any of it, mainly because he didn't remember most of it.

"I think I was drinking vodka that day, most of the bottle, pretty sure I blacked out. I kinda remember getting arrested, that's about it."

Now the hard part. "Do you know what you're looking at?"

"The PD [Public Defender] said I was never getting out. That's not right, not for this. Those dump trucks work for 'the man,' they don't care about people like me."

Having started my career as one of those "dump trucks"—I was offended.

"The truth hurts, but it doesn't change the facts. You have three strike priors, two prison priors, and two new robbery counts, with no real defense. You can't testify because you don't remember what happened, you'll be impeached with your prior convictions, and voluntary intoxication never works as a defense. Unconscious or otherwise, jurors don't really care once they hear about your prior record. The public defender may not have much bedside manner, but he was telling it like it is."

Rico became angry, I saw it in his face. I had dashed his hope.

"Murders don't get that kind of time, and I didn't hurt nobody. What kind of justice system is that?"

"One neither one of us agree with, but it is what it is." My tone was aggressive; I wanted to see if he would back down. I was not taking this on if I had to fight with my client the whole way. Been there, done that, it's miserable.

"Come on, Mr. Dunn, there has to be something you can do for me. I'm really not a violent person, an addict, yes, and a thief, but I've never really hurt anyone."

I scan his record again, "What about this ADW [Assault with a Deadly Weapon] with a gang allegation?"

"Oh, that was a long time ago, just young punk crap, hit a guy with a stick in the park, he was alright. Hey, how come they can use that against me? That happened long before the three strikes law, what's up with that?"

"Just another one we lost on appeal. We did win one recently, the Romero case—it says a judge can dismiss your strike priors if he concludes it is in the interest of justice to do so."

Hope made its way back into Rico's demeanor. I realized he gets angry when he is afraid. I could feel my heart softening—not the direction I wanted to go. It was time to leave.

I stood, still holding the receiver to my ear. I didn't want to talk anymore; I knew what I was going to do.

"Thank you, Mr. Dunn, I know you don't have to do this, God bless you, sir."

The "sir" was a bit much, but I would take it—maybe it would play in front of a judge.

Julie McCormick is my DA. I hate taking on prosecutors like Julie, It's hard enough slugging it out with some dude who is used to being a punching bag, but fighting with a woman, especially a total pro like Julie, is something I dread. Actually, it's worse than that—Julie is smart and hardworking, and to top it all off, a good person. She started a couple years after I did, so we crossed swords before, never to my advantage that I can recall. She will eventually tell me "No" politely and remind me of "office policy" and then say "where you going with this one, Phil, I thought you got into private practice so you didn't have to take all the losers."

That's what really hurts, using my own words against me. I'd get mad if I thought it would do any good. So, once again, I was reduced to professional groveling.

"Oh, come on, Julie, you don't want to try this case just because there's no offer, you've got to give me something."

"What's the defense?"

"Voluntary intoxication," I say as if I mean it.

Julie smirks at my bravado. "Good luck with that one."

"Look, Julie, he didn't hurt anyone, he was too loaded to even run away, thirty-three to life for this, really?"

Her demeanor softened. Unlike most prosecutors, she is not without a heart, that's why she's so good—she actually cares about doing the right thing.

"You know it's not my call, but I'll see what we can do. What's he looking at if we strike a couple of the old strikes?"

"Sixteen to twenty-three years at 85 percent ought to be enough time on this one." I'm almost desperate now, letting her know I'd take any deal I could get.

"We'll see," she said with a little smile. "Do your Romero motion and I'll run it past the powers that be."

Our conversation concluded, I nodded to her in humility, knowing she would help if she could.

Romero v. Superior Court was the first recognition of the brutality of the California ballot initiative that made any new felony conviction punishable by twenty-five to life in prison if the defendant ever suffered two violent or serious felony prior convictions.

It is safe to say voters didn't understand that the third felony conviction didn't have to be serious or violent to warrant a twenty-five to life sentence. Countless press reports about defendants getting twenty-five to life for things like stealing a pizza, a petty theft with a prior, making it a felony, educated the electorate. Many years later two initiatives overwhelmingly passed modifying "Three Strikes" to apply to only a third violent or serious felony, but in the interim the damage was done.

California went on an incarceration binge unlike any state in history quadrupling its prison population until the United States Supreme Court finally decided California's prison overcrowding amounted to cruel and unusual punishment. The Romero decision by the California Supreme Court was the first case to modify "Three Strikes," allowing judges to strike prior felony convictions if the court determined it was "in the interest of justice" to do so. This was Rico's only chance.

Prosecutors in every county, but particularly in conservative ones like Ventura, are very reluctant to give a deal to a three strikes defendant. They don't want to take the risk that he will be released someday and commit a new violent crime. If that hits the press, someone's career is over. Better to not ever take a chance on a convicted felon. Thus, the rationale for the pizza theft prosecution and countless others like it.

Romero made it possible for courageous judges to intervene on behalf of justice, the punishment should fit the crime, by dismissing a prior strike making a just sentence possible. At the time of Rico's case, the Ventura D.A.'s office would review letters submitted by defense attorneys seeking dismissal of "strike priors." They considered factors such as the significance of the prior convictions, age, competence, lack of maturity of the defendant, or the trivial nature of the new offense. Rarely did they agree to an outright dismissal of a strike. Rather, on occasion they might agree to "not object" to the judge dismissing a strike if the defendant pled guilty to the new charges.

After submitting my letter, and filing my Romero motion on Rico's behalf, I finally got a call from Julie McCormick. "We won't object to the judge striking two of the strikes, leaving him with one strike, if he pleads guilty to both new robbery counts, he's looking at a minimum of sixteen."

"That's sixteen at 85 percent, Julie, a whole lot of time for this..."

"Beats forever, after trial. Thought you'd be grateful." Her tone was aggressive.

"Don't get me wrong, I do appreciate it, Julie. I know it's not easy." I bit my lip to say no more.

"Go do what you have to do, Phil, and don't disappoint me."

I chuckled at that, as I knew it was said in good humor. "Of course not, Julie, I'll go see him as soon as I can."

I could tell Rico was anxious when I saw him waiting for the steel door to roll open. He moved quickly to sit on the other side of the thick glass separating us, and reached for the receiver.

"How are you, Rico?"

"Scared, if you want the honest truth, Mr. Dunn. I've been waiting a long time to hear from you."

"Sorry, they are never in a hurry to decide these things, but I do have a little good news for you: they have agreed to let the judge dismiss two of the strike priors, leaving you at sixteen to twenty-three, but I think the judge will give you low term, so sixteen years at 85 percent."

Rico's face turns red, the gansta' in him comes out: "That's crazy, for that crap, I didn't do anything to nobody. Sixteen years for getting drunk and being stupid, I ain't taking that deal."

Then *my* anger rose. It took a lot of groveling to get here and I didn't appreciate the attitude. "Look, Rico, you have no choice . . . a jury won't know the sentence you're looking at, just that you threatened those girls and took the money, then it's thirty-three to life, got it?"

Sorrow replaces anger as Rico slumped back on his stool so low I'm afraid he would fall off.

I have often wondered what other professions require its participants to deliver such bad news: "You have cancer stage four. If you live, you'll be miserable; otherwise, you'll die, lots of pain regardless"—that's what the patient hears. How do you have a bedside manner with such news? Reality is brutal; only thing worse is denial. I have no patience with denial, so I have no bedside manner—perhaps I should try harder. No, false hope is dangerous. It may make him feel better for now, but it's much worse in the end. It crushes a man's soul, leaves him weak and vulnerable, a dangerous state of mind for someone about to do a long stretch in prison.

"So, look Rico, the DA's going to expect you to take the deal at the next court date. She thinks she's doing you a favor. We don't need to make her mad by messing around with this."

"My mom . . . I can't tell her this, she thinks I'm going back to the men's home. She prays for me, for you, all the time, she's heard all the stories, she believes in you, Mr. Dunn."

"I'm not a magician; I don't pull rabbits out of a hat. I have to deal honestly with the facts, and the law, and with you.

I can't lie to you, give you false hope. It just makes it worse." Rico was near tears now; his tough guy exterior had been beat out of him by his attorney.

Pity made its way into my heart. "Okay, look I'll get a letter from the home admitting you. You've been in jail sixteen months actual, plus a year in the home. I'll ask the judge to strike the third strike. Theoretically he can do that, but it isn't going to happen, Rico. Don't start hoping for that one, it doesn't work like that, man. No judge has that kind of courage."

Rico recovered; it is the glimmer of hope he prayed for, the chance he might not go back to prison. He believed in miracles—even if I did not.

Maria Ramirez wasn't about to give up on any of her children, even Rico. He may have broken her heart countless times, but none of that mattered. She knew his true heart and would never stop fighting for it. She tried to discipline him when he was young, but with no help from his father, and having to work to support the family, Rico grew up wild like so many other kids in the neighborhood. As he came into adolescence, she pleaded with him not to be out all night, hanging with the homies in the 'hood. It didn't work . . . Rico started drinking when he was twelve, and doing drugs at thirteen.

First a "wannabe," then a "hanger-on," then jumped into the neighborhood gang, Rico's course in life was set like so many before him. Rico wasn't sixteen before Maria Ramirez retreated to the last refuge of defense of her child: she prayed for him unceasingly. Throughout all the years of bitter disappointment, she never gave up. There could be no abandonment of her child, no protecting herself from the agony.

The prayer warriors I have known like Maria Ramirez have always unnerved me. Giving it all to God is not my nature, I'm too into self-reliance. My faith is not that strong.

Rico's day of reckoning was upon us. His case was assigned to the Honorable Charles "Chuck" McGrath, a conservative "law and order" judge. like most all of them. In California, like other politicians, judges have to run for re-election every six years. In most counties the most powerful elected official is the District Attorney, particularly on criminal justice issues. The last thing any judge seeking re-election needs is the district attorney to handpick one of his deputies to run against a "soft-on-crime judge." That judge is in for the fight of his life, better to color within the political lines drawn by the DA than risk your judicial career on a criminal.

Chuck McGrath was different. He won his seat in an election, and better yet, he comes from the gentrified farming community of Ventura County. Anyone driving the 101 Freeway through the county likely would see a sign for "McGrath State Beach," an obvious statement of his family's generosity and influence in the community. Judge McGrath was intimidated by no one, and he would let this sentiment be known from time to time. Better yet, I knew him to be a practicing Irish Catholic, a conservative judge with plenty of his own political clout. That's as good as it gets.

The elevator from the holding cell arrived with Rico and a deputy guarding him. As Rico shuffled his way to the small bench where I was seated, I recognized the hollow look of the truly desperate. Dressed in "jail blues" with a white T-shirt, plastic sandals, and shackles around his ankles, he wore the uniform of the truly damned. It is much easier to punish people set apart from the rest of us—wearing chains reminds us, "he must be dangerous."

Motioning Rico to sit on the bench, I waited for the deputy to go back down the elevator. "How yah doing, Rico?"

"I've been better, didn't sleep much last night."

"Sorry to hear that, okay so, let's go over what we can expect to happen today. You plead guilty to two counts of robbery and admitted to having suffered three strike priors and two five-year prison priors. The DA won't object to the judge striking two of the strike priors by finding it is in the interest of justice to do so. That leaves you with a minimum of sixteen years and a max of twenty-three. I think under the circumstances he'll give you the low term of sixteen."

"I'll be an old man when I get out, if I get out alive."

A familiar tone of hostility comes with Rico's words. My response is standardized, "Look, Rico, I don't make the laws and I don't create the facts. Your PD told you, you were never getting out, I got you a deal where you're getting out someday. That's as good as it is going to get."

"My mom came to visit me last night. She told me God promised her, saying to me, "Mijo, you won't go back to prison . . . He told me you won't do one day in there."

Wow, just what I didn't want to hear. I thought I had set this up better than that—time for another healthy dose of reality. "So, when God tells me the same thing, I'll believe it, Rico. Until then, we need to stay real here."

Pain—the kind that comes with the loss of hope—took over Rico's face. A moment passed in silence as I tried not to let him know I shared his pain. I needed to remain strong; weakness would only make it worse.

"So, you're not going to try, man, didn't you tell me it's possible, that he could strike the third strike and give me probation?" Rico was pleading now, a reflection appears in the corners of his eyes.

"Sure, Rico, I'll take a hook shot from half court, but don't expect it to go in."

As visible tears formed, I couldn't help myself: "Alright, I've got an argument, unconventional as it may be, and we got the Victory Outreach crew out there for you. They've given the judge a letter telling him they want you in the home, so yeah, we'll give it a go."

"Yeah, man, you've got to go for it, I didn't have the heart to tell my mom, she thinks it's gonna happen. I can't be the one to break her heart again.

"She told me she got invited to a new church Sunday, a little place off the Avenue. The pastor did an altar call for those in need of prayer—she went forward, got down on her knees. A little girl, maybe twelve years old, came up and laid hands on her and told her, 'This says the Lord your God, 'do not weep for your child anymore, because I have chosen him to glorify myself through him.'"

This was way over the top for me. I didn't know if I should feel more stressed or just laugh it off.

"Look, Rico, you know I'm good with that, but I'm really afraid of disappointing a whole lot of people sitting in that courtroom looking for some kind of miracle. I've been crushed too many times, Rico, I can't go there anymore—it hurts too much. I'm just going to do the best I can for you, and not get caught up in everything else, okay?"

"Right, Mr. Dunn. I got it, it's dangerous to have hope, faith in things unseen. Just like prison, it's best to give up your hopes and dreams for the future, and just accept the brutal reality you live in, hope just makes you weak . . . vulnerable."

"Yeah, that's it, Rico, I guess, something like that anyway. So, you ready to get this over with?"

I stood, moved to the door, and knocked so the bailiff would know I want to come out. I heard the large jailhouse key clang into the lock and turn before the door was pulled open.

"Give him a couple of minutes, Pete, and then let the judge know we're ready." McGrath's bailiff was a kind man—a veteran of the system—and he could tell I was distressed.

"No hurry, Phil, whenever you're ready."

I looked out upon the gallery past the bar separating "us" from "them." It was packed with people all wearing their Sunday best. They were largely Hispanic of origin, but not entirely. All eyes shifted to me as the courtroom went quiet, the principal actor in this play had come on stage. Seated front row center was Rico's family, Maria Ramirez, Cecilia and Rico's little brother Eddie, who is now a Victory Outreach pastor. They looked upon me with expectation, hoping I would tell them something, anything, good about what is about to happen. I turned away, instead focusing my attention on Julie McCormick, who was seated at counsel table, looking confident as always.

I said to her, "He should be coming out in a couple minutes, then we'll get started."

As I sat down at the defense table, Julie leaned over and asked in a voice only I could hear, "So who are all your friends, Phil, didn't expect an audience."

"Just some relatives, and the Victory Outreach crew. You got the letter from the men's home, right?"

"Ahhh yeah, but that's not how this is going to go, Phil, it's not as if he's going to get probation."

"Well, you know, Julie, sometimes a man just got to do, what a man got to do."

"Okay, go ahead and put on a show for the family, but I'm going to argue for mid-term, just so you know."

Once again, I heard the clank of metal on metal as the extra keys on Pete's chain banged against the steel custody door, then the turn of the lock before the door swung open. Rico emerged, with Pete in escort. Rico, as trained, kept his hands clasped behind his back, and his strides short so as not to pull the shackles tight. Reaching the chair next to me, he waited for Pete to pull it out before sitting. The look in his eyes, and every other aspect of his demeanor, revealed the terror of the moment. Forbidden from making contact with anyone, verbal or otherwise, Rico never once looked out upon the audience.

"Remain seated and come to order. Court is now in session." Pete's call to order was a little stronger than usual—he had civilians to look after.

Chuck McGrath was never in a hurry. He came through the solid wood door behind the judge's bench and made his way up the steps to his chair as if it caused him difficulty. I knew better, despite being in his mid-sixties he was still an athlete. At about six foot two, thinly built with only a hint of gray in his light brown hair, he was still cutting a formidable figure. His appearance was softened by plastic-framed glasses and a casual demeanor. All of this was a trap for unwary lawyers who might be fooled into believing it was all very routine for this judge. He was paying close attention, even if he pretended otherwise.

"So, let's call the case of <u>People v. Ricardo Ramirez.</u> It would appear both sides are ready. Mr. Dunn, I'll hear from you first."

"Thank you, Your Honor, let the record reflect Mr. Ramirez waives arraignment for judgment, and stipulates there is no legal cause as to why judgment cannot now be pronounced.

"Your Honor, the Court will note we have filed a Romero motion as to Mr. Ramirez's three strike priors. I believe the People will not be opposing the dismissal of two of these priors, which would leave Mr. Ramirez with one strike, plus two five-year prison priors which are required to be served consecutive to the low term of six years, that is three years doubled with the one strike for a minimum of sixteen years at 85 percent. Under 1385, the court has no authority to strike either one of the five years prison priors, so that is why we have a minimum mandatory sixteen years here, at 85 percent should the court only dismiss two of the three strike priors. However, should the Court find it is in the interest of justice, it can strike all three strike priors thus, making Mr. Ramirez eligible for probation."

"Amen," Pastor Ramirez said loud enough for everyone to hear. Pete glared at him, but let it go.

"Sixteen years at 85 percent on these facts is a sentence we might have seen in medieval times, or perhaps in a novel by Victor Hugo about the French Revolution. It is absurdly harsh, brutally excessive, and thus in a word, unjust."

"Amen," again, but Pastor Ramirez was not alone this time; it was a collective "amen" coming from the assembled parishioners, followed quickly by "Quiet, court is in session." Pete was doing his job, but I heard a tone of restraint in his voice. I could tell McGrath was amused—a tiny smile formed at the corners of his lips before Pete's admonition swept it away.

"The punishment should fit the crime, regardless of someone's record. Getting absurdly drunk and demanding money from a couple young ladies who only call mall security to get rid of a pathetic nuisance, may technically fit the definition of robbery, but it doesn't justify throwing a man's life away." I heard a "that's right" from the back row.

"Mr. Ramirez only recently backslid into a ditch by starting up drinking again. Up until then he had many years of sobriety, having become a respected member of Victory Outreach, so, they are still here to support him. They believe in Rico, as they believe in the value of every soul that comes through their doors."

"Amen!" in unison this time.

"Alright, ladies and gentlemen, that's it, that's my last warning, I'm going to be removing people from the courtroom if this keeps up." Pete stood now. I've seen him bite before when he had to—this was his best professional bark. McGrath revealed no displeasure; he was no more intimidated by a crowd than anything else in his courtroom.

I snuck a peek over my shoulder and noticed my parishioners were properly chastised. They were running on instinct.

Now that they knew better, they wouldn't want to be disrespectful. We were in white church from now on.

"Mr. Ramirez has done sixteen months actual and what we are proposing is that he be given credit for time served, and an additional hard year in the Victory Outreach Men's Home as a condition of probation."

I saw Julie wince as if she didn't believe I would really say it. "He will spend a year getting up at 4:30 in the morning to study the Bible, pray, work all day for his church and community, then more church at night before lights out, and then get up and do it all over again. The type of personal and spiritual discipline needed to save a man from the pit that has become our prison system. Your Honor, the absurdity of the law in this case allows for but one just option, a grant of probation with no prison time, credit for time served, and a year at Victory Outreach.

"I realize what I am asking of the Court is an extraordinary remedy, one my client has no right to hope for. He is, in his current circumstances, much like the iconic literary character Jean Valjean of *Les Misérables*, who after spending seventeen years in prison for stealing a loaf of bread, was released back into the chaos and tyranny of French society during the revolution. Forced to wear the yellow vest of the parolee so people would know his status, he was shunned by everyone he met, and left to wander from town to town searching for scraps to eat. One night, having been denied food and shelter everywhere else, he lay down on a bench in the village square. There, someone took pity upon him.

"'See that light over a doorway there, that is the home of the bishop. Sometimes he will take in men like you.'

"Tired and beyond discouraged, it was only the freezing cold motivating Valjean to knock on the bishop's door. The maid answers and upon seeing Valjean, she attempts to slam the door shut, but the bishop is there. Grabbing the door, he gently tells her, 'No, no, invite him in, take out the good silver for dinner, and make up the bedroom, as we have a guest staying with us tonight.' The maid, near despair, goes back inside to do what it is she has done countless times before."

"At dinner Valjean is a crude beast, eating with his hands. Valjean says little, eats ravenously, when offered more he stuffs it in his one bag for later. He barely grunts his appreciation, and maintains a demeanor of confusion and hostility, so unaccustomed to acts of kindness is he. Suspicion and fear control his every thought. When led to the bedroom and shown the finely made bed, Valjean is speechless. The bishop can do nothing more than bless the man as he shuts the bedroom door behind him. Valjean attempts to sleep upon the mattress, but it is to no avail. Seventeen years of sleeping on the ground makes it impossible. A vision of the silver plates haunts his thoughts as he calculates their worth. Eventually, the temptation is too much; Valjean rises from the bed, goes to the dining room, and shoves all the silver plates into his bag."

Out of the corner of my eye I saw a mixture of amazement and panic take over the features of Rico's face. He had never heard one of his attorneys talk like this before, and as he would later tell me, "I thought you were losing it, I wanted to stop you and tell the judge I'll take the sixteen years, this is not my fault! I was afraid he would max me out after having to listen to a story that made no sense to me."

"His bag stuffed with silver, Valjean leaves the bishop's home in the dead of night. The weight of the heavy bag slows his escape. In the early morning he is spotted by a constable making his rounds, who never lets such a man pass without inspection. Discovering the silver, the constable confronts Valjean, who barely mutters the story, 'The bishop gave it to me.'"

The point of my story was drawing near as I paused to draw a breath, the awkward silence in the courtroom shot pangs of fear through my veins. *Am I making a fool of myself? Will any of this make sense? Gone too far now, have to see it through.*

"Brought in chains to the bishop, the constable expects a reward as he explains the details of Valjean's capture. Valjean never looks up, his head cast down in shame. He is resigned to his miserable fate.

"'My good man, you don't understand,' the bishop's tone carries the authority of his high office. "'Yes, I did give him the plates, but Jean, I don't understand . . .' The bishop pauses as he walks to the dining room table and grasps the ornately cast silver candlesticks. Taking one in each hand, he turns to Jean, who in amazement looks up to catch the bishop's gaze and hears, 'Jean, I gave you the candlesticks as well, why didn't you take them?'

"Mesmerized by the moment, Valjean cannot speak, only out of self-preservation does he extend the palms of his hands to receive the gift. The constable, stunned and dejected, bows slightly to the bishop and slips away quietly through the open front door.

"Now alone with Valjean, the bishop moves closer to the man he has set free and places his hands upon his shoulders saying, 'Today, Jean, I give you your life back, to live for good, and not for evil. Take the candlesticks and go in peace.'"

My moment had finally arrived, and I paused for dramatic effect—the line was loaded and ready to be delivered.

"You see, Your Honor, today you stand in the shoes of the bishop, the candlesticks are in your hands—you can breathe new life into this man or take it away, the choice is yours, Rico Ramirez's life is in your hands."

Having concluded, I sat at the counsel table, but Judge McGrath was still looking at me. His professional demeanor intact, he glanced in the direction of my client. Rico was appropriately humble; he understood enough to play his part perfectly.

"Ms. McCormick, let me hear from the People." Julie jumped to her feet; she was not happy with me.

"Your Honor, we all know Mr. Dunn is a great storyteller, but this one has nothing to do with the facts of this case."

Oh, how I hate a good comeback. Couldn't she just let the moment linger a little while longer? The parishioners were disturbed as well; they shifted uncomfortably in their seats, stiffening for the oncoming verbal assault.

"The defendant didn't just steal a loaf of bread," Julie continued, "he terrorized two young girls over a prolonged period of time, until they gave him what he wanted, money—money taken in a robbery by force or fear. Mr. Dunn's remedy might make some sense if this was his first offense, but his record indicates he is nothing less than a career criminal."

Lord, how I hate that label. It might as well be: "Trash, ready for disposal."

"Not just two strike priors but three! It's a gift that we are not objecting to the Court striking two of them. He really should be facing thirty-five to life, he's earned it. His record dates back to the age of thirteen, first the hall, the county jail, and two previous prison terms, this defendant doesn't get it. The People think this is a mid-term case plus the two five years priors, and the other enhancements for a total commitment of eighteen years. Submitted, Your Honor."

That was mercifully short, but brutal nonetheless.

The judge looked intensely at Julie and asked, "Ms. McCormick, is it the People's position that the Court does not have the authority to strike either of the five-year priors, because when I looked at this case, it seemed to me that would be the best way to arrive at an appropriate sentence in the matter."

Julie didn't like this question.

"That's right, Your Honor, under 1385(b) the Court is specifically prohibited from striking a five-year prior listed in Penal Code 667, thus the minimum sentence is sixteen years."

"Well, the People could agree to dismiss one or both of the five-year priors, couldn't they?"

Julie's face flushes red as she deals with the judge's challenge. "Yes, that is legally possible, but would violate office policy and is completely inappropriate in this case."

There was but a flicker of a flame in Judge McGrath's eyes but no discernible change in tone: "So since the People will not strike either five-year prior, in order to reach a sentence the Court deems appropriate, I will need to consider striking the third strike, correct?"

Julie was noticeably angry now. "The Court is not seriously considering—"

Wrong thing to say to this judge.

McGrath cut her off: "Oh yes, I think that's exactly what we are going to do. I find that based upon the facts and circumstances of this case, and the record now before me, that it is in the interest of justice to grant the defendant's Romero Motion as to all three strike priors, and thus I order them stricken."

The courtroom was covered in silence. Time was standing still. "Having made that order, Mr. Ramirez is now eligible for a grant of probation. I once again find that it is in the interests of justice to make such a finding, and at this time release Mr. Ramirez from custody, on a grant of five years formal probation with credit for 482 days actual time served. As an additional term the defendant is to serve the first year of his probation in the Victory Outreach Men's Home of Oxnard, California. Mr. Ramirez, do you accept probation on those terms?"

Rico, mouth wide open, turned to me and whispered, "What do I say?"

"You say yes, Rico, and thank you."

"Thank you, thank you, Your Honor . . . ahhhh, yes, I do . . ."

"Well then that will be the order, seeing no further business before the Court, we stand adjourned."

McGrath got to his feet quickly, pushing the large black leather-bound chair behind him. He turned and agilely stepped down from the bench, opening the door to his chambers and disappeared without making eye contact with anyone in the courtroom. His abrupt departure caused bewilderment in the gallery—a buzz of excited chatter grew as the more astute observers explained their interpretation of what just happened.

Rico, still in disbelief, turned to me and asked, "What's it mean?"

"We won, Rico, you're not going back to prison. In fact, you're getting out today, going back to the men's home . . . don't screw it up this time, okay?"

Rico was speechless. He understood what's been said, but he didn't dare believe it.

I looked at Julie. The anger had passed, she just softly shook her head. Her eyes caught mine and she almost smiled. Turning away, she collected her file and made her way out the back of the courtroom.

The clamor in the courtroom continued to grow. Since court was no longer in session, Pete didn't interfere. The audience members approached him for an explanation. Pete replied, "Judge released him, he should be processed out in three or four hours, you can pick him up at jail reception." Pete was smiling now—he loved it when his judge did something like this.

The assembled parishioners turned to me for further explanation. "Rico will be released in a few hours, you need to pick him up at the jail and take him directly to the Men's Home, no stops along the way. He needs to stay there for an entire year before he can go back into the community. Thank you all for coming, it really helped a lot."

"Thank you, Mr. Dunn and God bless you." It was Rico's brother, the pastor, speaking for them all. I was humbled by their appreciation, but it passed quickly. Realizing the glory of the moment, and the result, I felt a large "S" come up on my chest. Barely containing my exhilaration, I began making my way out.

"Forgive me, I have another courtroom to get to." Polite and respectful to a fault, they cleared the pathway letting me pass.

I was fully consumed with my own brilliance. I couldn't wait to tell my colleagues about this one. Passing through the foyer, I pushed hard on the handle opening the heavy oak doors out into the hallway. Outside, my stride quickened as I turned right to make my escape. Then I could go no further . . . On their knees praying against the wall, surrounded by the faithful laying hands on them, were Cecilia and Maria Ramirez. I do not understand the words, but the tears and shrieks of joy say it all. They know who made this happen, and they are not about to forget Him.

The "S" vanished from my chest as I recalled what must have been prophecy: "Do not weep for your child anymore; because I have chosen to glorify myself through him."

I recalled how I scoffed at that prediction, and when it came to pass, I sought to take credit for it. Humbled for the first time, I turned and placed my hand upon the shoulder of the man nearest me, and joined them in prayer.

I no longer remember what was said, or how long the prayer lasted, but the joy of that moment still resides within my soul.

CHAPTER FOUR

Super Cop

As I look back now, I realize John Jenks and I were made for each other. We looked as though we were cut from the same cloth. John—thirtyish at the time, a couple years older than me—carried himself with a self-righteous arrogance consistent with his all-American boy good looks, and all the accolades he received as an undercover narcotics detective. We were both true believers, convinced justice was on our side. He was mistaken, I was not.

I noticed one of his cases for a motion to suppress the evidence alleging he detained and arrested my client without sufficient probable cause. His arrest was for, "under the influence of a controlled substance," a misdemeanor carrying a ninety-day minimum mandatory sentence. My client was young, perhaps twenty, Asian, and attractive in a petite sort of way. The fact she tested positive for cocaine was irrelevant—the issue was not guilt or innocence, rather the unlawful conduct of Detective Jenks, a violation of a citizen's Fourth Amendment right against an unreasonable search or seizure.

Our judge for this hearing was Judge Fred Jones. Like almost all the Ventura County Municipal Court judges, he came out of the local district attorney's office. Before that he was a special agent with the FBI. Square-jawed, powerful build, and baritone voice, he ran his courtroom with an iron fist. Even so, I didn't think he was all that special. All the judges took a turn at trying to intimidate me into compliance, yet I was confident he would fare no better than his brethren.

The issue in the case came down to whether Detective Jenks engaged my client in a "consensual encounter," from which he then gathered sufficient evidence to arrest her, or had he arbitrarily detained a citizen otherwise engaged in lawful activity based on little more than a hunch. It was around midnight outside a bar in the city of Port Hueneme.

According to Detective Jenks he just walked up to her in this "high crime area," and struck up a conversation about the weather or some such nonsense. When speaking with her, "I recognized common indicia of recent cocaine ingestion, dilated pupils, she spoke rapidly, and appeared to be perspiring despite the fact that she was scantily dressed on a cool summer evening."

It was all the same old garbage I'd heard before, as if he did a medical examination on the spot. Then the DA had something more for me. "Mr. Jenks, have you been specially trained as a drug recognition expert?"

Oh no, not a DRE [drug recognition expert], do I have to listen to this again, Jenks is an expert, trained by other law enforcement to spot a drug addict a mile away, not just some beat cop, a super cop.

Jenks waited for the question to end and then turned to look me in the eye, smugly explaining each law enforcement "class" on the effects of street drugs on the human body and the "outward manifestations of recent ingestion." As he droned on about how many arrests he made, and how they were all convicted, I realized he was talking straight at me. He wasn't trying to convince the judge, that was too easy, he was trying to convince me. Now he had my blood up.

"Detective Jenks, isn't it true that you have been elected president of the Ventura County Narcotics Officers Association four times?"

"Objection, that's irrelevant."

"Sustained." Judge Jones made the DA flinch as though he was being admonished for breaking the rules. Jenks showed a bit of disappointment, revealing a certain vanity I might later exploit on cross-examination. His direct examination was by the book, though Jenks pontificated more than most officers; he enjoyed testifying.

"Mr. Dunn, you may cross-examine."

I got to my feet and started with, "Good afternoon, Detective Jenks."

"Good afternoon, Counsel."

"Now on the date in question, at midnight, isn't it safe to say it was dark outside?"

"That's correct."

"And there are no street lights in the immediate area where you contacted Ms. Hairo, correct?"

"Yes."

"Are you aware of Ms. Hairo's eye color?"

"Brown."

"Isn't it true, Detective Jenks, that it is more difficult to observe pupil size of a suspect in dim light when the subject has brown eyes?"

"That is true, but there was plenty of lighting in the area."

"From what source?"

"The lighted sign above the bar, and windows from inside." Jenks smiled, as if to say, *You got to do better than that, Counsel.* He was good, no doubt about it.

"Did you take her pulse?"

"No, I did not."

"Never met her before that night, correct?"

"Correct."

"So, you didn't know her manner of speech, how fast she normally speaks?"

"I didn't need to, it's always the same. She talked a lot, very quickly, just like everyone else I've encountered who is under the influence of a central nervous system stimulant."

"Isn't it true, Detective, that you suspected Ms. Hairo of drug use almost immediately upon contacting her?"

"Not immediately, but shortly after I was able to observe her demeanor, the physical symptomology."

"How long did that take?"

"Not long—you know what, Counsel, I've been at this so long, arrested so many drug addicts, I can pretty much walk down a mall and pick out an addict, out of everyone else in the place. Give me a couple minutes with 'em and I can tell you what they're using." *Wow, he's gone off script now, the cockiest cop I've run across.*

"Really, you can just pick them out of a crowd?"

"That's right, Counsel, maybe you should do a ride-along and I'll teach you how it's done."

Judge Jones chuckled at this—he was enjoying the show, at my expense. I decided to try a little different tactic.

"Now, Detective Jenks, you told us Ms. Hairo was scantily clad, just what did you mean by that?"

"That's not relevant." Judge Jones wasn't smiling now, he was indignant.

"Are you making your own objection, Your Honor?" I'd been told when Fred Jones starts rubbing his temple, I'd better look out for what comes next. He was doing a double temple rub now.

"That's right, Mr. Dunn, and it's sustained."

"I believe the Court heard the detective testify that Ms. Hairo was scantily clad, and his observation of her perspiring on a cool evening was a factor in his analysis that she was under the influence, so it's clearly relevant."

Jones slid his chair forward, putting his hands on the bench and leaned forward. That was one big dude up there and he looked really angry.

"Mr. Dunn, you're bordering on contempt here, I know where you're going with that question, and you are not going to try and dirty up a fine officer of the law with a sleazeball question like that. Your question is prejudicial, and sustained as irrelevant. Move on, Counsel?" Wow, he looked like he was ready to take me out to the parking lot! He could have done it too.

The sheer volume of his dress-down was good enough, but I'd never heard a judge go from zero to contempt that fast. *I can't back down here, can I? Can't let them think they're getting to me.*

"Very well then, what about perspiration, on what part of her body did you notice she was perspiring?" Jenks looked amused and was about to answer, but Judge Jones stood to his feet.

"That's it, we're done. This hearing is over, your motion to suppress the evidence is denied, there has been ample evidence presented justifying both the detention and the arrest of Ms. Hairo. Mr. Dunn, don't you ever come back into this court-room until you've learned how to behave like a professional. Detective Jenks, you're excused as a witness, with the thanks of this court and the community you serve. Motion denied; this court stands adjourned."

It pains me to admit it, Judge Jones got to me good. It wasn't so much the strength of the words he used, but the sheer power and authority with which they were delivered. Even Jenks looked upon me with pity as he shrugged his shoulders and stepped down from the witness stand. Even worse, my poor client was terrified. "I just want to plead guilty, and do the ninety days, don't make him any madder. He'll take it out on me."

Her fear was understandable and caused me great shame. I was there to protect her, to advocate for her, and now she felt betrayed. "Can I still take the ninety days?"

Pulling myself together, "Yes, we're going back to another courtroom, a different judge, tomorrow; that judge will let you take the ninety days."

"Good, that's what I want to do, I don't want to come back here, not with you as my lawyer."

It took me awhile to process the whole experience. It felt so personal.

Not long after that, I heard Detective John Jenks was awarded the Ventura County Peace Officers Association Medal of Valor. He was called out to an apartment about a disturbed man with a gun. When he got there the man was brandishing a rifle and screaming angry profanities throughout the building. Jenks described it like this: "His mother opened the door; she looked absolutely terrified. She tells us, 'My son has lost his mind.' I should have dropped him first thing, but his mother was right there, I couldn't shoot him in front of his mother. So, I just talked to him until he looked away for a second, and then I charged him. I managed to wrestle the gun out of his hands and arrest him."

I also heard Judge Jones was at the banquet, and he brought his two young sons along to see what a true hero looked like. After the banquet, Fred Jones came up to Detective Jenks and introduced them to him. He asked Detective Jenks if he would "autograph the program for my boys."

« « » »

I managed to go a couple years without again challenging Detective Jenks. I did see him around the courthouse, if he wasn't testifying, he was coming out of a judge's chambers with a search warrant. Colleagues shared similar experiences about him, essentially how he was untouchable and knew it. Then the myth unraveled.

I first heard about it in the courthouse, then I read the story in the *Ventura Star Free Press*. Detective John Jenks was arrested. A defendant withdrew his guilty plea, and was insisting upon a trial. The DDA assigned to the case called Jenks and told him the pound of cocaine he seized, had to be tested and brought to court as evidence. Jenks couldn't do that; he'd already checked it out of the crime lab. He didn't return it, he smoked it all.

Learning this, Lieutenant John Hopkins of the Port Hueneme Police Department got a search warrant for Jenks's residence. He was John's mentor, a friend who took pride in the exploits of the brash young detective. Now he was searching his home, and it didn't take long for them to find evidence of how Jenks's addiction had been running amok for a while.

Throughout the house and in his garage, they found evidence boxes holding countless plastic bags with only a trace of cocaine left inside. They also found hypodermic needles, various smoking devices, and thousands of dollars in cash. Midway through the search, Lieutenant Hopkins left the scene and went to his car. He didn't go back in, he just sat there and cried.

I celebrated Jenks's downfall. Their self-righteous superstar was exposed as a hypocrite, and they would be forced to admit it. They might even begin to understand we all have feet of clay, anyone of us could fall from grace. Perhaps they might begin to accept that mercy has a place in the criminal justice system.

My righteous indignation continued until I happened to be walking past one of the arraignment courts one morning when I noticed a slew of reporters waiting outside. My friend and personal mentor, George Eskin, was representing John Jenks; and when I saw him exit the courtroom, I knew what was going on. George gave a brief statement before Jenks (who made bail) came out of the courtroom. George ended with a request that they let his client leave unmolested, as he would not be making a statement. It was not to be.

As soon as Jenks walked out, the camera shutters went off and the reporters surrounded him. Just as he managed to break free, a man I recognized as another narcotics detective stopped him in his tracks. Detective Ivy was a scary-looking guy—tall, thin, shoulder-length blond hair, scraggly beard, and lightly tinted sunglasses. Ivy had a nasty reputation with the defense, not only was he known for his lack of candor on the witness stand, but some lawyers were genuinely afraid of him. "The kind of guy who would drop a bindle of cocaine in your pocket when you're not looking." That's how one of my colleagues put it.

Jenks had nowhere to go as Ivy drew close to him, offering what looked like quiet words of sympathy. Then he reached up and put his hands on either side of Jenks's face, pulling him in, and kissed him on the lips. It was straight out of *The God-father*, the kiss of death given to a traitor. Jenks managed to break free, but he was obviously shaken by the experience. His public humiliation wasn't enough, or the prospect of being sent to prison—now he must live with a symbolic threat upon his life.

Everything changed for me in that moment. I saw John Jenks the man, not the rival. I took no pleasure or amusement in Ivy's dramatic display, rather it appalled me that sworn law enforcement would so easily and publicly behave like a mafi-oso. Jenks became one of us, a broken man coming to grips with what it was like to stand in the dock with all the power of the state focused on punishing him. His former colleague wanted retribution, the complete destruction of the man.

There it was again, compassion. I buried it deep within me, but now it erupted within my soul. My competitive instincts bested by an emotion I could not deny. As my heart softened, I slowly came to grips with my own cruelty. I self-righteously celebrated another man's pain; I enjoyed his suffering. Given the right circumstances, I sought retribution; I was no different from those I condemned as hypocrites.

Prior to his arrest John finally admitted his addiction and went into recovery. Had he not, he would not have survived. His addiction was exacerbated by the fact he had unlimited access to the drug. Most addicts are limited in their use, since as their addiction worsens, the unraveling of their lives leads to loss of employment and the funds to purchase more drugs. Other criminal activity may compensate for the loss in the short term, but inevitable arrest and imprisonment interrupt the addiction spiral. John didn't have to pay for his drugs, and he was able to hide his addiction from law enforcement because he was one of them.

John's issues with drugs and alcohol started early and likely were inherited. Alcoholism ran in his family and he found out as a young man he had an enormous tolerance. "I was just twenty when I graduated from the academy. Once I got out on the streets, I started going to cop bars. We called it 'choir practice,' you know for the choir boys, anyway I could stay out all night. It was nothing for me to put away ten or twelve Long Islands, or two six packs, before going home.

"Drinking was one way of dealing with the stress. I became a cop to help people, but what you find out is often there's nothing you can do for them. Like the first motorcycle accident I went to, the guy's head was shaved off by the tree he ran into. Scenes like that stay with you."

They also have an effect on your personal life. Four years out of the academy he married Pam Scholle. "A beautiful girl, five eight, slender with plenty of curves, brown eyes, brown hair, I still wonder what she saw in me. Quiet, strong, and loyal, she's everything I'm not. I told her before we got married: the job came first, and she was okay with that. She didn't know how bad it would get, but she never stopped loving me."

Likeable and ambitious, John rose quickly through law enforcement ranks. At first, he was by the book, "I rolled up on a scene where they had some guy on the ground cuffed, and the senior officer took out his flashlight and started pounding on the guy. I said, 'You can't do that!' He told me, 'Learn something, rookie, he hit one of us—better to get some justice now, we won't get it later.'

"I wasn't very big when I first went out on patrol, maybe 145 pounds. I pulled over this ex-con, big dude, been lifting weights in prison. He had a warrant out, I told him I was going to arrest him. He said, 'Oh no, you're not,' and he hit me so hard he broke my jaw. That's when I got into power lifting. I went from 145 pounds to 185."

John's philosophy also shifted. He went from wanting to help people, to "putting the bad guys away, it was them versus us. I started wearing sap gloves, the kind with lead stitched into the fingers. If I hit somebody, they were going to stay down."

There were other traumatic events that helped solidify John's view of the world. "I got a call about a woman heard screaming inside an apartment. When I got there, I opened the door and immediately saw a blood trail that led me through the living room to a balcony doorway where I found her face down in a puddle of blood. She'd been shot five times with a .357 magnum. Three in the stomach, one in the head, and another in the chest. I carefully turned her over and found she was still alive. I tried to stop the bleeding, so I was covered in blood. When I got back to the station my commander told me I needed to go to the hospital and get a dying declaration about who the shooter was. That required me to ask her 'You know you're dying, right?' I got the name, but telling her that was cruel. Then, remarkably she lived, and I heard she was really angry about me telling her that—that really tore me up."

John started having trouble sleeping, often reliving traumatic events in his dreams. His way of coping was to engage in extra-long choir practices. Alcohol provided some temporary relief, but it also interfered with sleep. "Some nights I wouldn't get home until four in the morning. I'd sleep maybe two hours, get up, and get right back out there."

John likely was suffering from what today would be called Post Traumatic Stress. Lack of sleep, the relentless stress of the job, and the traumatic events he endured all contributed to this condition. Another symptom developed as well—a form of paranoia called hypervigilance. "I decided I needed to be invincible, so strong bullets would bounce off my chest. That's when I started using anabolic steroids. I got up to 235 pounds, and I was bench pressing 350."

Still, deep inside John were roots of his original purpose. He wanted to help people, not hurt them. "After I made detective, and started working drugs, I noticed I was arresting the same people over and over again, mostly for cocaine. Most of them weren't bad people, more pathetic than anything else. I started wondering what was so great about the stuff that people would ruin their lives over it. I had a quarter pound I seized, so I decided to snort a line. I loved it. All the stress, the fear, the insecurities went away. I spent most of the night snorting cocaine. When I woke up the next afternoon, I was as depressed and ashamed as I had ever been. I put a gun in my mouth, but then I remembered it was still there, in the detective's file cabinet. I knew I could kick those blues; that's how it all started."

John functioned well as a newly minted addict. The drug suppressed feelings of anxiety and anger that boiled over into his personal life at times. His relationship with Pam got better. In general, he seemed to be a happier person. The problem is the body develops a tolerance to the drug, so more has to be ingested to achieve the desired effect. That, or a better delivery system has to be used. In the beginning it was called "freebasing," the process of synthesizing cocaine base into a smokable drug. The tiny "rocks" it formed became known as "crack."

Crack cocaine is probably the most addictive substance ever developed by man. It's high is immediate and intense, the ultimate feeling of euphoria, invincibility. But it doesn't last long, and the letdown is equally dramatic. So, in order to get back up, the user has to smoke more. It's as insidious a substance as has ever been created. It tore apart the inner cities of our nation in the 1980s, and its sale and distribution is what fueled the proliferation of criminal street gangs.

Unfortunately for John, he knew all about freebasing. With unlimited access, and a growing need for the drug, it was inevitable he'd give it a try. "I'd be sitting in my unit smoking cocaine, thinking if I get caught, I'm going to prison. Then

I'd look at the coke and think, *As long as I got this, I don't need anything else.* One time while I was smoking it, I blacked out. I wake up, see the car's drifted out of the lane, and I see my shirt's on fire. I pulled over, doused the fire with a beer, and shook my head and thought, *That was a great high*—and lit the pipe right back up again."

John started to display all the classic signs of cocaine addiction, he lost forty pounds, he called in sick, his behavior was increasingly erratic. His commander asked about his personal life; John denied everything. Because of who he was, no one made the connection. He also took bigger risks on the job. "I was going into places to buy drugs without back-up. One time I'd made a connection with this old biker chick selling meth, and when I got there; there was this huge Samoan guy at the gate. When I got inside, she asked me if I wanted to try some. I told her, 'No, just give me an eight ball.' She didn't like that, she kept insisting I try it, and the Samoan guy was lurking around behind me.

"Then she says, 'I think you're a cop.' I told her, 'Look, I'm on parole, if I test dirty, I'm going back to prison, this is for business.' She tells the Samoan guy, 'Search him for a badge or gun.' I had a miniature tape recorder in my front pocket and a .380 in my back pocket. I got mad and told 'em to forget it, and I started for the door. Then she says, 'Take it easy, you know I can't be too careful.' I gave her $225 for the meth, and they let me go, but they could have taken me out. That one shook me up—I could have died over an eighth of an ounce.

"I knew the madness had to end, and I figured what better way than getting killed in the line of duty. Since it didn't happen, I just kept spiraling down. I'd go into the detective's office in the middle of the night, rock up and smoke all night. I was like the lab rat that chooses cocaine over food, the end was coming one way or another."

John did have something to hang on too, a reason not to end it all. Pam stuck by him; and now there was Whitney, and soon there would be Connelly. Pam saw what was happening, eventually she reached out to John's friend Mark Riddering.

"Mark was a godly guy, he tried to hold me accountable in the truth. He was working narcotics in Ventura, and we had come up together, so we saw a lot of each other. Even when he knew what was going on, he was never judgmental. They both worked on me until I finally surrendered. I checked into Hope Recovery Center up in Santa Barbara County.

"My counselor was Relly Nadler, he had been with Outward Bound, so I could relate to him. I had to learn a lot about myself, mainly that I was a selfish jerk. I had delayed development like most addicts. Once you quit using, your personality reverts back to when you last lived life sober.

"It took me three weeks, but when I got there, I wanted to get out and save the world again. Riley said, 'Whoa now, you've still got a lot of work to do . . . you've got to figure out what got you here in the first place.' I wasn't going for it, but then I got the call from the DA's office. After that, they served the warrant on my house. I had nowhere else to go, but jail.

"When I finished the program, there was a warrant for my arrest. I turned myself in. The booking officer was an old friend, J. T. Samuel. J. T. was a gruff old-timer, tough as nails. The kind of cop who never played politics. He never got promoted past senior deputy; now he was just booking in new prisoners at the jail. J. T. didn't want to book me, said he couldn't do it. I told him, 'I did the crime, J. T., I got to get booked.' He booked me, but there were tears in his eyes when he did it. That really touched me. I realized other people cared about me, and they were hurt too."

John's criminal case was assigned to Judge Fred Jones. This may have been a coincidence, but I doubt it. Perhaps George Eskin managed to maneuver it into his courtroom, maybe the judge had something to do with it. I had long since gotten past my original conflict with Judge Jones. I came to realize our original encounter was something akin to pledging a fraternity or boot camp. Once initiated, my respect for him grew as I realized he really was a courageous and honorable man. Still a little on the punitive side, but not afraid to rule against the prosecution when it was the right call.

The courtroom was packed on the date of John Jenks's sentencing. The district attorney filed only one count of grand theft; a felony punishable by a maximum of three years in prison. George Eskin argued for probation, a sentence that might include a year or less in the county jail, but no time in prison. Unlike most criminal defendants, John was able to present abundant character evidence on his behalf. Mark Riddering wrote for them all when he said, "I hate the sin, but I love the sinner."

Most of John's law enforcement colleagues stood with him, some did not. John later learned Detective Ivy contacted the probation officer preparing his report and told him he had informants who told him John had been selling drugs. The probation officer refused to include the accusation in his report. The district attorney asked for a state prison commitment due to the severity of the crime and the impact it had on other prosecutions.

Judge Jones sentenced John to five years on probation, no time in jail, and credit for time served in a rehabilitation program. I was flabbergasted by this sentence, as were most of my colleagues, whether they were defense or prosecuting attorneys. After I got over my surprise, I realized this result was what I was advocating for my entire career. Now there was precedent for it—rehabilitation instead of prison. Mercy rather than punishment, for someone who deserved it. It could no longer be one size fits all: "do the crime, do the time." Life circumstances and future potential should now be considered for each precious soul facing a criminal sentence.

The redemption of John Jenks did not occur in a single moment. Rather, it was a process in which the faithful played different roles at different times. Many Christians feel they have not participated in "The Great Commission." That is, they cannot point to any one individual they evangelized who then chose to be baptized and became a disciple of Jesus Christ. But what we often forget is we are not responsible for the conversion—that's the work of the Holy Spirit. We are to be His hands and feet, to play our part when called upon. This was certainly the case for John Jenks.

"I grew up in a Catholic home, and I went to catechism, my mom saw to that. But when I went away to college, like a lot of us, I quit going to church. Then when I became a cop, and saw all the evil going on in the world, I rejected God. 'If there was a loving God, this couldn't have happened.' I made myself God, if I made myself strong and worked hard enough,

I would get all the bad guys. Still, the root was always there, waiting for others to water it."

Pam was raised a Catholic, and didn't believe in divorce. Rather she prayed for her husband, prayed he would become the man God meant him to be, the man she fell in love with.

"In my journey there have been so many, those that stuck by me through it all, and those that came along side me when I crashed and burned. Even you, Phil, you were one of the first to take a chance on me."

John's career as a cop was over, but his talent and expertise were still there. "I got a job selling cars, but I was no good at it. John Masterson, owner of Masterson Motors, took a chance on me, even before I got sentenced. I worked construction for a while, but it didn't pay the bills, then George hired me do a little investigation work on a case. Next thing I know Phil Dunn's giving me a call. That was a shocker. I got it though, I was still an expert—in fact I knew more about drugs than ever . . . I had personal experience."

John was a godsend to me, and the defense. He could testify for us as an expert witness, investigate our cases, and most importantly prepare sentencing reports providing "factors in mitigation," to be considered by the court at time of sentencing. The prosecutors and judges who so dutifully relied upon John's testimony before, were hard pressed to deny it now. Rarely, if ever did his fall become an issue, rather he was treated with deference and respect. As time went on, and his recovery proved total, he became a symbol of what was possible for any, and all defendants.

Most successful recovery programs use, to one extent or another, the Twelve Steps developed by Alcoholics

Anonymous (AA). Fundamentally, AA requires a recognition that "you are powerless over your addiction," and that successful recovery comes from recognition that there is a "higher power." It is well known the basic tenets of AA are grounded in Christian theology. Stripped away are all the ceremony of formal religion. AA meets the lost where they may be found, in a moment of personal crisis. AA meetings, and the honest testimonies of others who have suffered the same affliction, provide hope of recovery. It is within this environment where John's faith was first renewed, grew to new heights, and set the foundation for a life's work helping others recover.

"I started getting invitations to speak about my experience and recovery. First at local high schools, then at Youth for Christ, and even to training classes with LAPD. Youth for Christ was particularly good for me because I could share my testimony freely. After that, I felt comfortable talking about God wherever I went.

"I had learned to rely upon God and not myself. Self-idolization didn't work for me, it doesn't work for anyone. The more I realized it wasn't about me, the better my life went. I learned what it meant to be a good husband, father, and friend. I rediscovered the empathy and compassion within me, those beautiful emotions had always been there, but I had done my best to bury them. It didn't happen all at once, but with each troubled soul God put in my path, I was given the opportunity to do God's work. I started relying upon God's strength and understanding, not my own."

Of all the stories I have written, I think John's was the most difficult for me. I had long since forgotten what he went through. We still liked to harass each other about our first encounter, but what happened after that, no longer came into my consciousness. We have worked so closely together for so long—recalling the pain of his addiction caused me great sorrow.

When I asked John if he would consider letting me tell his story, he quickly told me, "If it could be used to help someone else . . . yes, I'll do it." The fun part was trying to remember all the cases, all the souls, we sought to put on the right path, "The Way." Neither of us kept track, we were no longer keeping score. As John told me, "That would make it about us."

What I can say about my friend is he has been enormously successful. He got his master's degree, got appointed to the panel of experts on drug and alcohol counseling with both Los Angeles and Orange County Superior Court, and is a qualified expert in Federal District Court. He is also known to be a drug and alcohol counselor "to the stars." We are all familiar with celebrity actors and athletes having issues with addiction, and though we are unable to be specific as to whom John has counseled, I can assure you the list includes some of the most prestigious.

"Those aren't the cases I like to work though, give me some homeless gal or a gang banger represented by the public defender. No sense of entitlement, not all self-involved. Give me some guy like Rico Ramirez, somebody who grew up in the 'hood. When I go interview them in jail, they can't believe it. 'You cared enough to come see me?' I've had the toughest bikers and homeboys, guys that have done years in prison, break into tears just because I asked them about their mother."

If anything, John is more of a zealot now than when we first met. There's no one he doesn't believe can be saved. As

I write this story, we are working on a case together, a young man facing a possible life sentence for a crime of violence. Of course, he's a long-term addict, and he was suffering from, "alcohol and cocaine delirium" at the time of the crime. John doesn't understand why I won't ask the DDA to give him probation; even though he was on felony probation for the same kind of violent crime when he did this one.

"He's a good kid, Phil, he just needs to get clean."

"Let's hope he gets clean in prison, John, and he doesn't have to stay there the rest of his life."

I have to remember John Jenks has always been, and will always be, a true believer. The difference now is what John believes is true.

CHAPTER FIVE

The Darkside of Criminal Justice

My first week as a newly minted deputy public defender, Steve Davidson—one of the grisly old lawyers who had a striking resemblance to Jack Nicholson in style and demeanor—called me into his office and told me to sit down. Then, he leaned across his desk, looked me straight in the eyes, and said, "Phil, there is just one thing you have to know about this business—do you know what it is?"

Not easily intimidated, even then, I thought for a moment and then recalled the standard responses I was taught, like "our job is to insure all of our clients' constitutional rights are protected," and "whatever you do, don't socialize with the clients."

"No, no, no, Phil, you don't know what you're talking about. The one thing to never forget is there are a lot of bodies on the battlefield out there, don't be one of them!"

I feigned appreciation to Steve for his concern, quickly got out of his office, and didn't go back for a long time.

It would be many years before I understood what Steve was trying to tell me.

《《 》》

Len and I were on a roll. It had been a very long time since we heard the clerk read the dreaded "guilty" verdict handed down by one of our juries. "Not guilty" is what we were used to hearing.

This one, <u>People v. Ricardo "Ricky" Gonzalez,</u> appeared to be no different. Ricky was looking at sixteen years for a double shotgun robbery in downtown Ventura, of a couple sitting in their car after dinner at a local restaurant. The suspects wore hooded sweatshirts pulled over their heads with bandanas over every portion of their faces except the eyes. Running up to the car, they leveled shotguns at their victims through the open driver's side window, demanding all their money, phones, and credit cards.

The whole incident probably lasted less than a minute, but the trauma of having a shotgun stuck in their faces was still apparent when they testified almost a year later. The woman in the passenger seat readily admitted she could not identify anyone; all her attention was focused on the shotgun barrel. The man, however, had a different story. When asked to identify his assailants, immediately he pointed to Ricky and his co-defendant and said, "Yes, there's the one who did it." This came as no surprise as he had identified them both in a drive-by lineup the night of their arrest.

Ricky and three of his friends pulled into the parking lot while the crime was still being investigated, and all of them fit the general description of the suspects. Immediately detained, a quick search of their van produced just one piece of evidence, an unfired shotgun shell. Ricky and his co-defendant were wearing hooded sweatshirts, the other two were not.

All four were lined up on the sidewalk as a patrol car with the victims inside slowly drove by using its spotlight to illuminate the suspects. Two officers stood behind the four men, and right before the patrol car arrived, they lifted the hoods of the sweatshirts on Ricky and his co-defendant. The female victim said nothing, but the man immediately picked out the two hooded suspects as his assailants.

Len was outraged by Ventura P.D.'s tactics, an obvious suggestive lineup violating every protocol he followed as a robbery detective with Oxnard P.D. Len had reached his limit of bad and sometimes dishonest police work. Conflict with his supervisor over it caused him to take an early retirement. Now he was a defense investigator relishing every opportunity to point out the error of his former colleagues' ways. This case was particularly exasperating for Len. From the beginning he told me, "There is no way someone can ID a suspect with a hood and a bandana on; while looking down the barrel of a shotgun." I wasn't convinced until Len ran a little experiment past me.

He came to court with a life-size poster board picture of a man with a hood and bandana on, and stuck it in front of me saying, "Do you get it now?"

"Get what, Len, it's a picture."

"Look again."

"Okay, alright, I guess I'm missing something, what's your point?"

"I knew you couldn't tell—you don't get it, Phil; the picture is of me."

Wow, I thought, *I didn't get it, but now I do*. I couldn't tell even when he was sitting next to me; this was one powerful piece of evidence. The strategy wheels of my mind churned as I contemplated how we might get this little demonstration in front of our jury.

The case was assigned to the Honorable Herbert Curtis III. Judge Curtis was a former prosecutor of course; at the time just about three-quarters of the local judges came out of the DA's office. Herb Curtis grew up in the inner city of Cleveland, Ohio. A track star in high school, he won a scholarship to Cleveland State University. Upon graduating he became a teacher by day, and a law student at night. After passing the California Bar, he took a chance on an interview for a position in Ventura County DA's office. Personable, athletic build, and quick with a smile, he had all the ingredients for a successful trial attorney. Hired after his first interview, Herb Curtis quickly earned a reputation as a formidable trial attorney and a capable manager. After a short stint in administration, he got appointed to the bench by Governor George Deukmejian in 1984.

I liked Herb Curtis personally; he was much more down to earth than most of the judges. He enjoyed talking in chambers and occasionally regaling us with a story about life on the streets on the east side of Cleveland, or what fight his uncle Don King was about to promote. Don King remains a legend in the boxing world to this day, and much of it was not pretty. Having been convicted of manslaughter as a young man, doing some time in prison, and then climbing the ladder of professional boxing to become almost as famous as Muhammad Ali, whose fights he promoted, Don King came up the hard way. Herb Curtis's relationship to the man gave me hope for my judge. Alas, it was not to be, though Herb Curtis was not a mean-spirited judge, he certainly was no friend of the defense.

He virtually never ruled for us on a point of consequence, and on one occasion I had him reversed on appeal on an issue the DA's office refused to contest.

Herb Curtis was also the only judge I knew who openly carried a gun. Strapped in a holster around his ankle was a .38 caliber revolver. When I once asked him about it, he told me, "I'm my own backup—if something goes down in the courtroom, the first guy hit is my bailiff. I'm not going to be second."

So, Herb Curtis wasn't a great judge to try a serious case in front of, but the pickings for the defense were slim. He might never give you a ruling, but at least he wouldn't ride you the whole way.

David Lehr was our prosecutor. Well respected, easy to work with and certainly not afraid to try a case, David didn't try to deal his way out of a tough case. I found David a particularly difficult opponent as he suffered from multiple sclerosis and quite effectively took advantage of his disability. Unable to move about the courtroom without the use of a cane, David developed a sympathetic charisma that was hard to combat straight on. His courage was evident; though in my opinion his success as a prosecutor had caused him to go over the top on this one. I hoped David had let a little complacency slip into his game.

Len knew David, of course, and since he was going to testify about other evidence he produced, pictures of the scene that night and so forth, maybe he could also mark the hooded bandana man picture like all the other photos. I cautioned him to make sure he showed it to David first, which he did.

I started Len's testimony with the routine stuff, laying a foundation for all of our pictures, and then, "Mr. Newcomb, let me draw your attention to defense exhibit "K". Are you familiar with this photograph?"

"Yes, I am."

Trying to keep my tone and volume the same as before, I thought, *Only two questions to go.*

"Mr. Newcomb, what does this photograph depict?"

"Well, it's a life-size picture of a man wearing a hooded sweatshirt, hood up, and a bandana over the lower half of his face." Len answered matter-of-factly. *Now, the coup de grâce.*

"And, how did you take this photograph?"

"Well, I set up a stationary camera, on a timer, put on a hooded sweatshirt with a bandana over my face, and took a photograph of myself."

I heard a slight gasp from the jury box, and noticeable shifting within their seats, but I couldn't resist one more question, hearing no objection. "So, this is a picture of you, Mr. Newcomb?"

"OBJECTION! Your Honor, I know nothing about this, counsel never told me this was a picture of Mr. Newcomb!" David at first looked embarrassed, but now he was angry, very angry.

Having prepared for the moment, I shot back, "We gave the exhibit to Mr. Lehr before marking it, is he admitting he couldn't tell it was Mr. Newcomb?"

Herb Curtis was not amused by our little demonstration. "Mr. Dunn, I will see you and Mr. Lehr in chambers—now!"

The back door heading to the judge's chambers was a few feet behind the jury box. Next to the door was the witness stand, where a large white board with magnets held up exhibit "K", facing the jurors. On either side of the white board were large wooden doors, when closed covered the white board. David, seated closest to the jury, lead the way across the well of the courtroom as we headed toward the door. When we got to the white board, he stopped, leaned on his cane, and reached over to close the doors on each side of exhibit "K". Seeing this, I hesitated, and in perhaps my best moment of courtroom theatrics, shrugged my shoulders and shook my head a little before heading through the door.

In chambers Judge Curtis wasn't buying my argument. "This is not admissible evidence, little more than a cheap trick, certainly not an admissible demonstration, even if Mr. Lehr knew about it."

"Cheap trick." Now it was my turn to be offended. "Len gave it to him, we had it marked, it's not my fault he couldn't tell who it was." Things were getting ugly, and I could feel the pressure growing as the judge considered greater sanctions than simply ruling exhibit "K" inadmissible.

"You might want to consider a mistrial, Mr. Lehr, because we all know that once the bell has been rung, no admonition from me is going to unring it."

Horror gripped me. I had a winner going here and now they were plotting to steal it from me. I changed my tone, pleading, "Come on, David, you can't want to do this one again." David hesitated, thought for a moment, then said, "No, let's finish it, I'll just use it against you in argument."

Back in front of the jury, Judge Curtis in his sternest voice announced, exhibit "K" is ruled inadmissible; all of Mr. Newcomb's testimony on exhibit "K" is stricken from the record. Ladies and gentlemen of the jury, what that means is that none of what I have ruled inadmissible is evidence in this case, and therefore, it is not to be considered by you in any way in your deliberations."

As the judge spoke, I watched my jurors intently. Predisposed to like, or at least respect his authority, confusion now reigned over their faces. They had always heard it was the defense that got away with suppressing evidence, but here the prosecutor's objection was sustained, and the judge was telling them a truth they witnessed should be ignored for some unspoken reason. For a few of the more independent jurors a certain discontent came across their faces as they chafed under the oppressive nature of the judge's order.

My closing argument was based upon a false identification of two young men who happened to be in the wrong place at the wrong time. As I delivered my summation, I could tell most of the jurors were with me. Asking them to consider the gravity of their decision on a young man's life, I saw my likely foreman, a Hispanic man in his mid-sixties, nod in agreement as I told him, "This decision, your verdict, may be the most consequential decision you will ever make affecting another person's life." The facts, as they played out in court, made it possible to argue with righteous indignation building to a final call to do justice on behalf of Ricky Gonzalez because, "if you do not, none of us are safe from this kind of prosecution. Do what is right . . . muster up within yourselves the moral courage to find Ricky Gonzalez not guilty of all of these charges."

It didn't take them long, perhaps three hours. The reading of the verdict was, as always, extremely intense. With the first "not guilty," I knew we would get to hear those beautiful words spoken into the record three more times as both defendants were acquitted of all the charges. Each time the precious words were spoken, a cheer came from the gallery as the friends and family of the accused could no longer contain their joy.

It was as good as it gets.

« « » »

I didn't hear a word from Ricky until almost three months later. I ran into him in the courthouse one morning. Seeing me he walked over to shake my hand and apologize "for not getting a hold of you, to thank you earlier." Ricky didn't look good, since he had been in custody prior to, and throughout the trial, he had the pale but clean look of someone who wasn't getting any sun, but had no access to drugs or alcohol. That look was gone as he had clearly lost weight, and his demeanor was consistent with so many of the drug addicts I represented over the years. *Methamphetamine most likely*, I thought.

Three months later Ricky walked into a liquor store in Ventura with a shotgun, held up the clerk, and before leaving, he shot him with the shotgun. He didn't make it. The local paper reported the clerk left behind a wife and three children.

After the shooting, Ricky grabbed a rifle, put on body armor and barricaded himself in a house. The Ventura SWAT team surrounded the house, and when given a clean shot, they shot Ricky dead.

« « » »

Herb Curtis retired as a judge in 2007. His retirement was premature as it was well known to have been related to a drinking incident in which he allegedly told law enforcement they better leave him alone since he was hearing one of their murder cases at the time. His personal life also appeared to be suffering as he went through at least two divorces. He did practice law to some extent as he joined a local criminal defense firm, but he chose not to ever appear in front of his former colleagues. So, we never saw him around the Ventura Courthouse.

On February 6, 2017, police were called to Herb Curtis's home—neighbors reported shots fired. When they arrived, he barricaded himself inside while his girlfriend lay bleeding out from bullet wounds. Hostage negotiations ensued as Ventura Police sought to confirm the shooting victim was still alive. Additional shots were then heard, so the SWAT team broke down the door just as Herb Curtis shot himself to death.

«« »»

In war they call it collateral damage. The unintended consequences of battles fought in an endless struggle known as the criminal justice system. Those of us charged with doing justice within this adversarial system are not immune to its consequences. No, far from it, the horror of it all is not experienced in a catastrophic moment as in war, but rather it is a slower form of torture administered in small doses over decades of exposure. A form of Post-Traumatic Stress, the result of witnessing so much suffering with no ability to alleviate it. For some, a temporary salve is administered in the punishment of the convicted, but the satisfaction is short lived. It is a never-ending cycle of pain and retribution.

As for me, I always feared the day I learned I had successfully defended someone who went out and did it again, or as in this case, worse. When it happened, the war still raged, so

I had little time to absorb the impact. Still, it will always be there, lingering somewhere inside my conscience—a constant reminder of the dangers of self-reliance, the limitations of our own understanding. I've learned the hard way. It is better to seek God's will in our lives, than rely upon our own perceived wisdom, no matter how right it might seem at the time.

CHAPTER SIX

God Runner

It was a Monday, 8 a.m., and I was sitting in a Calimax parking lot in downtown Tijuana, Mexico. I didn't want to be there, and I didn't want to go where Jorge Garcia was going to take me. I guess I was there because I was first introduced to Jorge by Chuck Colson. It was at a banquet at the Nixon Library in Yorba Linda. I didn't want to meet Chuck Colson, but Rose prevailed upon me to go because "what you're doing is a lot like what he's doing." I really didn't think so—I was trying to keep them out of prison, not turn them around once they got there. I was taught prison was an evil place from which no one ever really returns.

It was more than that though—Chuck Colson looked like my father, a little under six feet, crew cut, dark horn-rimmed glasses, always at least a sport coat, shirt, tie, and wingtip shoes. They were part of the generation before me—you know, "The Greatest Generation"—except my father didn't live up to that ideal. He left my mom for another woman just when I was coming of age, and hadn't spoken to me or my sister for thirty years. We all carry around our own little bag of prejudice.

I tried to stay away, but Chuck Colson came to me. "I have heard good things about you, Phil, your work in Mexico, and your approach to criminal defense. You know I did some defense work myself before I got indicted."

Wow, this isn't what I expected. "Ahh, thank you, Mr. Colson, that's very kind of you."

"Call me Chuck, please." He extended his right hand and I shook it; his grip was firm like other Marines I've met. At least that was consistent with my stereotype.

"Have you met Jorge Garcia? He's our director of Spanish Ministries." Jorge was shorter than Chuck, thinning jet-black hair combed back, tinted wire-rimmed glasses, the kind that darken in the sun, and a pressed collared shirt proudly displaying the PF (Prison Fellowship) logo. His handshake was soft, consistent with his humble demeanor.

≪ ≪ ≫ ≫

A late-model Ford sedan pulled up next to me, bringing me back to the present. Jorge smiled through the windshield and got out with, "Brother Phil!" as a greeting. "Jorge, it's good to see you." We give each other a hug; I pick up a hint of his cologne. Jorge was beaming, he had finally triumphed over my fear of the mission to come.

"What we're going to do is load up on supplies before we go in. Soap, toothpaste, toilet paper, that sort of thing, then we'll give it to the men when we get inside." The Calimax was enormous . . . think Walmart. We loaded up four baskets of basic hygiene essentials, checked out, put it in the Ford, and drove to La Mesa Federal Prison. It didn't take long before we turned onto a side street and pulled into a small parking lot in a suburban neighborhood.

I'd been there before, almost thirty years earlier. Our church was supporting a mission known as Dorcas House, named for Dorcas in the book of Acts, "who was always doing good and helping the poor" (Acts 9:6). Rose was with me then, and we brought our children—Rebecca, age five, and Peter, age three. That's right . . . we brought our kids with us. You see, we were throwing a party for the children of La Mesa. The children of the prisoners, along with their mothers, were allowed to live inside the prison with their father. Rather than splitting up the family, they kept them together, a Mexican rehabilitation program. The downside being children were growing up inside a prison.

It was a village from the Middle Ages. Everywhere on the perimeter a twenty-foot cinder block wall with razor wire at the top, with observation towers intermittently placed, looked down upon a hard dirt square covered with small shacks, makeshift tents, and an occasional building used by the guards. Along one wall stood a series of small storefront shacks serving as local restaurants and stores. Everyone moved about freely, the guards didn't control anyone's movements, they mainly hung out along the walls. Smoke lingered in the air from various cooking devices creating a particularly detestable stench when mixed with the accumulated garbage spread throughout the yard.

In the center a large kettle hanging from a tripod of sticks sat unattended. "It's what the prison makes," I was told. "Only the most destitute eat from it, they say it's uneatable." Now I knew why we brought so much food with us: burritos, tamales, fresh vegetables, and gallons of fresh water. The fun part was we also brought a bag of toys, ice cream, and a birthday cake for the children.

We were escorted into a building covered with a tin roof at a far corner of the yard. Walking in I scraped the top of my head on a low-hanging rafter, which only added to my anxiety. Once inside, everything changed in the moment. All the children of the prison were seated in a circle on the floor surrounded by their mothers. Their excitement was palpable, and it turned into muffled shrieks of joy, as they caught a glimpse of the toy bag.

Rose sprang into action; her teacher training knew how to handle this crowd. Soon they were organized into various groups playing Duck, Duck, Goose, while the rest of us set up for the party. Before long she had both groups of kids playing together as if they went to the same school. When the game ended, the excitement level rose another notch. The expression on these kids' faces chased away my fear, and replaced it with joy. Then, I got to play Santa Claus. There are no words to describe the face of a child receiving her first doll, teddy bear, or truck.

It was thirty years ago, but the memory was still fresh. I half hoped for a similar experience this time, but I knew better. The war on drugs, cartel violence, and the explosion of the prison population in both our countries, left no room for rehabilitation on either side of the border. The other thing I knew was La Mesa was bigger now, not in physical size, but population. Originally designed for 1,500 inmates, it currently held more than 7,000.

The guards outside the gate looked ominous, but as soon as they saw Jorge, everything changed. I didn't understand the greetings in Spanish, but Jorge explained we "were fast-tracked through security, but before we went in, the warden wanted to see us." Escorted to her office, in transit we picked up Pastor Lalo and Eric Prager. Lalo was in charge of Baja Christian Ministries prison ministry, and Eric, the son-in-law of the ministries founder, Baja Bob, its new executive director.

Jorge received a big hug from the warden as we entered her office. Then she broke into English for my benefit. "Please sit down and tell me who and what you brought us today."

"You know Lalo and Eric, of course, and this is brother Phil, he's a lawyer in California."

"Welcome," she smiled sweetly.

"Thanks for having me."

"Well, Jorge, the men will be happy to see you. What you do really makes a difference."

The conversation went on like this for a short while, and then slipped back into Spanish. I continued to marvel at the reception Jorge received. Left with my own thoughts, my mind wandered. *They must know Jorge's history*, I thought, *his record, this isn't how it would go down on the other side of the border. We're not so forgiving, no matter how much good you've done.*

Jorge grew up the oldest boy in a family with seven children in the Colonia Libertad just outside Tijuana. His parents were "very poor, dirt farmers in Mexico. When I was twelve, they decided to move us across the border. My father had a job at the Hotel Del Coronado, busing tables. We lived in Imperial City."

Jorge didn't adjust well to the change in culture. "I didn't speak any English, and the schools at that time didn't help us out much. In fact, I had one teacher who use to make fun of me in front of the other kids, when I tried to speak English. He even used a ruler on me, right across my knuckles."

It wasn't long before Jorge started getting in trouble. He wasn't very big, "but I was good fighter. One time this bully was picking on a girl, I knocked him down, one punch. That made me real popular with the other kids. Unfortunately I learned that violence can earn you the respect of others.

"I started hanging out with the wrong kids, my parents worked all the time, so they didn't know what I was doing. We stole bicycles, sniffed glue, gasoline, stupid stuff. By the time I was in the eighth grade I was staying out all night, quit going to school, then I went to Juvenile Hall. Got in a fight in the barrio, the other kid got stabbed, I only did ten days for that, but I learned about claiming your 'hood; we were 'Imperial' or 'South Side.' I became a soldier in a war for the streets of San Diego County."

Inevitably, Jorge was drawn into the drug trade. Juveniles, under the age of eighteen, receive significantly lighter sentences on drug offenses than adults, so drug traffickers recruit them as distributors. "I was bringing kilos of marijuana over the border, I'd just leave the car in a parking lot, I got $120 a delivery, that was a lot of money for a fifteen-year-old in those days. Then my uncle got me in deep; he was hooked up with what would later be known as a 'cartel.' Before long we were taking four trucks a day over the border, that was 320 kilos a day. I got as much as $5,000 a trip. I saved some of the money, but most of it I spent on cars, and my habit. I was into everything—pills, cocaine, heroin, LSD, you name it, I did it.

"I started moving heavier stuff, more money in cocaine and heroin, easier to get across the border. Things were pretty easy in Mexico, I got busted one time with an ounce of coke, when I was nineteen, but we were paying the local police chief a thousand a month, so I got out of that one." The staggering profits in the drug trade made bribery a small part of the cost of doing business. "We found an INS agent we could pay off, $10,000 a trip across the border. It was worth it for the security—200, 300 kilos at a time, yeah it was worth it.

"This is about the time I got married, we'd been dating since we were fifteen, nice girl. She really didn't know about what I was doing, didn't ask. We had four kids, but I was too busy running drugs to be much of a father. I loved my kids, but I loved the drugs more. By the time I was twenty, I was totally addicted."

Jorge was thoroughly immersed in the dark world of drug trafficking. He hung out at night clubs, drove fancy cars, rented houses used to sell drugs, and started carrying a gun. "I had people working for me, even a body guard, the drugs make you paranoid. That and the money; people get greedy, you get ripped off, then you got to do something about it."

On one occasion, a car was left in a parking lot, but when the buyer opened the upholstery to get his 300 kilos; it was gone. "I was sure I knew who did it. I went to his house, had some of my people with me, we tied him and his wife to a chair. We beat on him a long time. I wanted my money. He didn't come up with it until I grabbed their son and put a .38 in his mouth. That's when he gave me the money."

By then law enforcement in San Diego knew all about Jorge Garcia, but they had a hard time making a case against him. "One time, they raided one of my houses, found a pound of heroin. My lawyer told me I was looking at state prison, but my guy that lived there took the rap. He said it was his and nobody else's. We paid his family $2,000 a month while he was inside.

"Then things started getting rough in the '80s. The cartels were going after each other, they wanted to consolidate the suppliers. They were moving tons of cocaine in one shipment." The myth that cocaine wasn't addictive took hold in America, and our appetite for cocaine knew no limits. Drug lords working mainly out of Columbia, were becoming some of the wealthiest people in the world.

"I went to a meeting in Guadalajara, and there was an FBI agent there—he was working for us. They had eight different planes they were using, flying in 200 kilos at a time. They didn't need to drive it across the border any more. I knew our time was about over. Those guys don't like any loose ends, you're either working for them, or you're a problem for them."

Whether out of fear, or drug paranoia, Jorge turned to the dark arts for protection. "There was a witch I knew in Mexico, she was only four and a half feet tall, but she was the real deal. She used tarot cards to predict the future, and voodoo against my enemies. We would meet at a mausoleum in the cemetery, she would kill a kitten and drink its blood. Horribly wicked things, I was totally consumed by darkness.

"There was only one time when the light shone through. A family friend, Manuel, he'd been after me to go to church.

He was so persistent I finally said 'yes'—I'd go one time, just to get him to leave me alone. I thought the people would sit there quietly, like the Catholic church I went to as a kid. But at Iglesia Nueva Vida (Church of New Life), the people stood up and sang, some were crying, rejoicing, it really touched my soul. Then they had an altar call. I went forward, I was crying, they laid hands on me, prayed for me. I went down to my knees, said my own prayer, 'God, You know I'm destroying myself, come help me.' It didn't last though, I got back to my car, made sure my gun was still under the dashboard, and started right up again. But a seed had been planted."

Jorge brought me back to the present: "Phil, time to go, they're taking us down to the yard." The warden led us to a hallway and then down some steps, where we waited for a guard to open the gate. We carried the Calimax bags filled with supplies, which were searched while we waited. The door opened into a hallway made of steel posts and chain link running along the side of the building. Though I retained a strong memory of La Mesa's "recreation yard," there was nothing familiar in what I saw this time.

Everything was concrete and steel. The yard was split in two, one section was filled with inmates either walking or jogging an oval pattern. Most of the older prisoners stood in groups along the fence. The other yard was hosting the world's largest soccer game. I marvel at the ferocity with which they play on concrete. The ball was tattered, as were most of the men's shoes, if they had a pair at all. I checked out the interior walls; they were solid cinder blocks twenty feet high. I, too, was amazed to think Andrew Tahmooressi had scaled them with his bare hands and feet.

As an exchange of prisoners on the soccer yard was completed, a gate opened and we were led between the two yards and into a cell block. As we entered, I was unable to see, as the bright sun outside was replaced by an interior room lit by just one bare bulb in the ceiling. As we passed through, the dank smell and a dripping shower head provided evidence of the room's purpose. Entering the cell block, I was confronted with the most desperate conditions I have ever seen human beings endure.

There are perhaps twenty cells in a row, and at each one of them, men come forward, reaching their hands out between the bars. I estimate the cells at about 20' x 30', each crammed full of men—most of whom are two, sometimes three, to a bunk. The triple-high bunk beds consumed most, if not all, the floor space in the room. Tattered blankets laid upon the cement, covering what I must assume are the weakest of the men. In the back, there was one open latrine, which required a major repositioning of all the cell's occupants for one of them to use it.

Jorge, Eric, and Lalo rescued me with instructions on what to do. "We need to divide everything up evenly," Eric told me, so we counted what we had in each bag. I carried the soap bag as Eric, who is fluent in Spanish, asked the men up front how many are in the cell. He told me, "Twenty-two." I am concerned that everyone gets a bar, but as I began handing them to the men, I noticed they were passed hand-to-hand to the back, until the last ones were kept by the men up front. We repeated the process with toilet paper, toothpaste, and some packaged food—each time the distribution was entirely equitable, no man went without, no man got more than his share.

There was little time to reflect, but in the back of my mind I realized I knew someone who did four months in one of these cells. Fighting a war in Afghanistan would be traumatic enough, I couldn't imagine what Andrew went through while he was in here. He at least was able to mount a defense, and his circumstances became known to the public. These men often wait years before their case is adjudicated. Like this prison, Mexico's courts are overcrowded. Many of the men have been abandoned by their families. They have no one else; it's as if Jorge, Lalo, and Eric are their only friends.

The supplies distributed, I wander down the hallway looking in on each cell, dodging inmate clothes hung from lines tied to the bars and the wall behind us. As I pass, I hear someone: "Phil—Phil, that's your name, isn't it?" I am trained not to respond to inmates clamoring for me, but this is different. I go back to the cell I just passed, I see a tall, blue-eyed, gray-haired man at the bars: "Don't you remember me?"

"No, can't say I do, what's your name?"

"Bruce. You visited me, remember?"

"I don't think so, I haven't been here in thirty years."

"I haven't been here that long, but your name is Phil, right? I'd swear you're the same guy that came to visit me. Maybe his name was Phil too."

Bruce extended his right hand through the bars. I was both perplexed and intimidated by the strangeness of it all, but I shook his hand anyway.

The cell block exploded into a deafening chorus of men singing. Lalo was leading the song. I didn't recognize the words, but I knew the tune: "Amazing Grace." It was impossible to think, let alone talk over the passionate plea of 200 men. I learned what "saved a wretch like me," sounded like in Spanish. My heart got the better of me; I feared Bruce would notice.

The entrance gate opened and a guard came in, leaving the gate open. Jorge said, "Our time's up here, but they said we can go into the HIV unit, so that's where we're going next."

Fear gripped me, but I knew it would do me no good to give into it. I was part of the mission, and there was no turning back.

"Well good luck, Bruce, and God bless you, brother."

"No, no, Phil, God bless you, and thanks for coming."

As I followed Jorge down the hallway, and out the gate, my rational mind tried to understand the paradox of Bruce. I failed to come up with a logical explanation.

As we waited in the corridor outside the cell block, Jorge warned me, "We may be here a little while, they're moving other inmates."

"Tell me, Jorge, are these the worst conditions you've seen?"

"Oh no, brother Phil, the prisons in Central America are the worst, Ciudad Varrios in El Salvador, with MS-13, that's bad."

"So why do you do it, Jorge? You could stay in the United States."

"You know, I was one of them, I was worse. When my wife divorced me, I really lost it—I lost my mind, I was doing more drugs than ever, injecting heroin, coke, you name it. My mom tried to help me, put me in a mental hospital. I was there twelve days, when they released me, they told me, 'You keep this up, you won't live another seven years.' I didn't care, when I got out, I started right up again."

"So, how'd you get it together, how'd you wind up here, doing this?"

"I was trying to kill myself, overdosed three times, but somebody always brought me back. I asked them, 'Why'd you help me? I want to die, that's why I overdosed.'"

"Well, *something* happened; you've come a long way back."

"I was running out of money, I was out of the game, and there were guys looking for me. I was desperate, finally I went back to that church, Nueva Vida. I cried out to Jesus, 'Save me!' I was crying, I never cried; I had a stone heart, but I felt His presence. My Lord and Savior answered my prayer. I felt like I'd been saved for something, my wretched soul had been forgiven.

"I knew I had to change my life, get away from everyone and everything. My family still had some land in Mexico, I went and lived there, four years. I had no money, lived off the land, but I was sober, and in my right mind. I read the Bible all the time, I made a commitment to God, to help others like myself. When I came back to the U.S., I was a changed man. I even got married to my beautiful wife."

"How'd you get in with Prison Fellowship?"

"I had nothing when I came back—the big-time drug runner didn't even have five dollars for a hamburger. I opened a janitorial service, God humbled me. I spent my days cleaning toilets. Then I started visiting guys I use to know, in prison, telling them about Jesus. That's how I learned about Prison Fellowship; I saw the volunteers going into prison. They told me they needed someone to work with the Spanish-speaking inmates, so I applied for 'Director of Spanish-Speaking Ministries.' I was told I was going to get the position, so I gave up the janitor business. Then I guess they looked into my past and changed their minds. I happened to be going into Chino one day, the same day Chuck Colson was there. I told him what happened. We were in the prison parking lot, he made a phone call, then he came back and said, 'You got the job.'"

"When was that?"

"It was 2003, been with them ever since."

"Jorge, I know you've been working with MS-13. I don't know that much about them, just the El Salvador connection, and that they came out of L.A. I guess originally they were providing protection from other gangs, for Central Americans?"

"That's right, they really didn't get so violent until the civil war in El Salvador was over. That's when a lot of them got deported. They got caught up with the former security forces, that's who taught them to be ruthless, hacking up people, going after families, women and children, bad stuff."

"You went to see those guys in prison?"

"Yeah, Ciudado Varrios, the worst place I've ever been. They run MS-13 out of there—they have a whole section of the prison the guards won't go into. They just slide food under the door. If someone dies, they drag him out and leave him outside the door. There's 1,700 men in there."

"You went in there?"

"Yeah, I had to go alone, they tried to talk me out of it. I just knocked on the door, told them Pastor Garcia was there to see them. They said they'd heard about me, so when they opened the door, they were all lined up on both sides of the hallway. Young kids, tattoos all over their faces, it was pretty intimidating. The 'leader' came up to me, asked why I was there, I told him, 'I came to tell you God loves you.' He thanked me for coming, he even told me about his family; so when I got to San Salvador, I rented a little storefront for his wife who sold vegetables. They had two little kids. So, when I went back, everything was good. I brought in some medicine, shoes, soccer balls—they couldn't believe it. I even helped them set up a little bakery. They made enough bread to sell on the street; they were very proud of it. They made me 'Spiritual Father' of MS-13."

That brought a smile to my face; I am proud of my friend. Chuck Colson sure knew what he was doing when he hired Jorge Garcia. "So, Jorge where else have you've been?"

"Bella Vista, in Columbia- now that one really shook me up. We were in there doing our regular ministry, when a couple of kids come up to me and say, 'The Boss wants to meet you.' I know I can't say no, can't disrespect him, so I said, 'Okay, set it up.'"

"How'd that go down?"

"They told me, 'Two guys will meet you at a shopping center in Medellin, at 6 a.m.' They said they'd be in a Suburban, and they described the guys. I didn't sleep much that night, but I figured I didn't have much choice if I wanted to keep working in Columbia."

"Where'd they take you?"

"After we got outside the city, they put a hood on me, so I don't really know where it was. It took about two hours—we stopped at a couple of their security check points and I could hear them talking. Finally, we stopped and they took the hood off. We were at this big beautiful hacienda in the jungle— swimming pool, horses, a gorgeous place. There were guys carrying automatic weapons everywhere, just like in the movies.

"Then El Jefe comes out . . . strong-looking man, about 5'10" maybe two hundred twenty pounds. He tells me, 'Pastor Garcia, I've heard so much about you, thank you for coming.' He takes me inside, sits me down in this big room, with his guys all around. Then he tells one of them, 'Go get the girls.' This guy comes back with all of these beautiful young ladies, he tells me, 'Pick one of them.' I replied, 'No, no thank you, I'm a pastor and I'm a married man.' I know he's testing me. He was alright with that; he sent them away."

"Then I hear him tell one of his guys, 'Get the suitcase.' The guy comes back and gives it to The Boss, he opens it and smiles. Then he closes it and turns it around and pushes it in front of me and says, 'Go ahead . . . open it.' So I open it, and it's filled with hundred-dollar bills. He tells me, 'That's $250,000, it's for you—your ministry, all the good work you've been doing.' I didn't want to disrespect him, but I know I can't take the money. A lot of people died for that money; and if I take it, he'll own me.

"The Boss, he laughs and tells me, 'Use it to help my people behind bars, buy them Bibles.' So, I try and tell him, 'I can't get it out of the country, they'll stop me at the border.'"

"He tells me, 'I can take care of that, just tell me when and where you're going over, it won't be a problem.'"

"So, I'm praying for the right thing to say, and then I just tell him, 'No, I just can't take it.' The Boss isn't used to people telling him 'no'—I can see he's upset."

"What—my money's no good? You know I love God too!"

"Then, it just comes out of me: 'You can't help God, but Jesus can save you. Just let Him into your heart, and everything will change for you, like it did for me.' El Jefe listened, but he didn't like what I was saying. He didn't want to change, at least not yet. I could see the rage in him; it kept growing."

I could see the anguish on Jorge's face as he remembered the moment. He paused to collect himself. "Next thing I know one of his guys comes up behind me—tells me it's time to go. He walks me down to a room, unlocks it, and pushes me inside. I can't see a thing, it's dark, and I hear him locking the door."

Once again, Jorge paused as the memory overtook him. I had never seen my friend show fear, but now he was searching for words. "I waited patiently, until, I cried out to God. 'I don't want that life anymore!' I told God, 'I'm ready to take the bullet, but please, God, protect my family.' I was begging, 'Jesus, save my family!'"

Tears filled Jorge's eyes. I felt bad making him relive it. Trying to move forward, I asked, "How long were you in there?"

"Maybe three hours; three hours of prayer, crying out to my God, 'Rescue me! Save my family, do not let the evil one triumph over your servant.' When you're in that kind of trouble, you really pray. I knew God was with me, but I still was afraid."

"So, how'd you get out of there?"

"Finally, the guy comes back, unlocks the door, and tells me, 'Come out.' He knows I'm scared; he doesn't like me, doesn't like the way I talked to El Jefe. So, he's pretty rough with me, keeps the barrel of the gun in my back until we get back to the Suburban. The Boss is there, shaking his head like he's disgusted with me, with what he's got to do. I figure they'll just march me into the jungle, shoot me there; no one will ever know what happened to me. Then he breaks into a smile, grabs me by the neck, and says, 'You really think God could love an outlaw like me?'"

"Yes, God loves all His children, just the same; so of course, He loves you."

"I tell you what, pastor, these men are going to take you back to Medellin. The money, I'm going to keep it here for you; you let me know when you need it."

"It was a long ride back, I really didn't know what they were going to do, where they were taking me. Finally, they took the hood off, and I saw we were in the parking lot in Medellin. That was the first time I believed I was going to be alright. I got out and they just drove away. I went straight to the airport, got the first flight to Miami. It took a while before I went back to Bella Vista."

I chuckled at this, just as a gate opened and a guard motioned for us to follow him across the yard. I hid my trepidation as best I could, as Jorge told me, "They don't always let us come in here, they lock it down when someone's too sick; but we really need to help them, most of these guys don't have any family left."

Once again, as many men as will fit squeeze up to the bars, their arms thrusting through them. The cry of, "pastor, pastor, *por aqui* (over here); *por aqui* (over here)," reverberated throughout the cell block. Eric and Lalo touched hands with the men as we make our way down the hallway. They stopped in front of one of the cells, and began fervently praying for each man they touch. I remained in the background, counting out bars of soap, toothpaste, and rolls of toilet paper. If anything, the cells were more crowded than before. I noticed some of the men were without shirts, revealing skin lesions and open wounds. Though I didn't understand their pleas, their gestures made it apparent: they were desperate to receive the meager supplies I possessed. I couldn't ignore them any longer. Starting with the soap, I gave it to the men up front, who passed it to the men in back, just like before.

As I approached each cell, I saw more deprivation than most have witnessed in a lifetime. Yet, amidst the obvious pain and sorrow, there was an inexplicable beauty present. Human kindness once given is contagious. It prospers amongst the most desperate of souls. I finally saw the prison for what it was; right there, in the moment, it was the holiest place I had ever been.

CHAPTER SEVEN

The Mailman

It's a Thursday, about 11:00 a.m. at Saint Andrew's Presbyterian Church in Redondo Beach, California. A group of about eighty men and women wait outside the fellowship hall. Inside parishioners have set up about twenty round tables and chairs, prepared racks of clothing, and various other stations providing shoes, personal items such as soap and toothpaste, and a closet filled with canned food.

Other parishioners sit at a table to assist in filling out applications for medical assistance, financial aid, and housing. But these goods and services are not why they wait outside—rather it's the hot food. Eggs for breakfast, ham and beans for lunch with all the salad you can eat, and donuts for dessert. With the opening of the church doors, a community of the homeless enter to be served by the church of Saint Andrew's.

The city of Redondo Beach is located in the South Bay of Los Angeles County. As a beach community it is one of the upscale neighborhoods in Southern California, a place where gentrification has remodeled most of the small homes built after World War II so, it is almost impossible to find a home for anything less than $750,000. Housing prices have driven up rental units as well, so a typical one-bedroom apartment goes for more than $2,000 a month. This reality, among others, is why Los Angeles County has more than 58,000 homeless people living on its streets—some in cars, others in tents, and still others have no shelter at all. Redondo Beach, with its temperate weather and long sandy beaches, attracts and retains its fair share of the 58,000.

California boasts the world's sixth largest economy, and Los Angeles generates the highest gross domestic product of any county in the nation. Homelessness however, remains an intractable problem despite all the money and attention it receives from the press and politicians. Citizens overwhelmingly voted to tax themselves more than a billion dollars with the landmark Measure H sales tax, but it has had little impact on the problem. Now the political situation has turned into a "crisis of mental health treatment" and a call by our governor to allow doctors to write "prescriptions for housing" and even involuntary confinement to insure "they" get the "treatment 'they' need."

What is rarely mentioned is the scourge of homelessness; like so many other societal ills, it is often self-inflicted—most commonly through drug addiction and alcoholism. Nowhere is this fact more self-evident than in the criminal justice system. Arraignment courts in Los Angeles and throughout our nation are filled daily with the incarcerated homeless. Defendants arrested for public intoxication, under the influence, and even misdemeanor vagrancy, pack the custody boxes of our courtrooms.

When I first started my legal career as a deputy public defender, these misdemeanors were taken seriously, some requiring a minimum of ninety days in jail, today they are routinely CTS (credit for time served), as there is no room in the jail for misdemeanor offenders. Even on more serious offenses, including felonies not requiring a prison sentence, offenders in Los Angeles County do approximately one day for every thirty days they have been sentenced to serve. Over-incarceration is symptomatic of the same disease driving homelessness—a societal spiritual crisis revealing itself in increasing numbers of addicts, criminals, mental health patients, over-doses, and suicides.

My quest for the day is not only to witness the success of another small band of Christians living out their calling to care for the least of us, but also to document another example of the cure for what ails us all. I am here to see Michael "The Mailman" Lee. He looks just like all the other parishioners, about six feet, blue eyes, and a decent head of graying hair for a man sixty-seven years old. His calm demeanor and humble manner serve him well when working with the homeless.

Saint Andrew's serves as the permanent address for about two hundred homeless residents of Redondo Beach. Having a place to pick up mail is a big deal for someone who doesn't have a mailbox. Letters from relatives, relief checks, health care, and government notices, and even responses from potential employers, all need a place for the postman to deliver. So, every Tuesday and Thursday, Michael gathers all the mail the church has received and distributes it to everyone who shows up at lunch time. If someone doesn't come for a while, Michael goes out looking for him. Michael is perfect for the job; not only does he know everyone, he also knows all the places in Redondo Beach the homeless live. He should . . . he was one of them off and on for thirty years.

Michael was born and raised in Redondo Beach, but his childhood was not as idyllic as most of his peers. He didn't meet his true father until he was sixteen, and that meeting only lasted long enough for the man to walk away asking Michael to "never trouble me again." Rather, he grew up in his mother's house, who had a parade of men come through when he was young, until she finally married a former police officer, still angry about losing his job over the theft of county-owned radios.

At age six Michael stepped into a crosswalk when the driver of a car stopped and signaled him to go ahead. The second car didn't see him and hit him straight on. When he regained consciousness, "My left leg was behind my neck." Taken to the hospital, "they put a cast on it, and sent me home that night. The pain was unbearable, and what was worse, my stepfather tormented me, calling me 'sissy'—things like that.

"I was crying all the time, I quit eating, and finally my mom took me to Torrance Memorial. The bones had never been set, and I had a massive infection. I almost died; they kept me there four months." Michael never fully recovered from the accident. Learning of it, I noticed he walks with a slight limp to this day.

"More than that though, the trauma, the pain, the memory of it is still there—that and the beatings. Most of the time he used a belt, a couple times he gave me a black eye with his fists. My mom, she never got involved. I don't think she was afraid of him; it just felt like she didn't care."

When Michael was eleven, he experienced homelessness for the first time. Tired of all the abuse, "I ran away, lived in a field in the neighborhood for about three weeks until somebody noticed me. I got picked up and sent home. I really got it that time."

Michael's problems at home turned into problems at school. Poised and well-spoken today, you would never guess he never finished High School.

"I smoked my first joint at eleven, did acid at fourteen—pills, whatever was on the street. That's when I quit going to school, ninth grade it was."

Michael did have one person who loved him, a grandmother in Oklahoma. "We moved around all the time, sometimes I'd just go live with Grandma. I didn't know anyone in Oklahoma, you know, have any connections, so I pretty much stayed out of trouble when I was with her. Knowing somebody cares about you when you're a kid makes a big difference."

When Michael turned sixteen, he moved back in with his mother and stepfather. He was stronger, big enough to fight back. The beatings stopped. "I thought we were getting along, but when a friend of mine hid some marijuana in the backyard, my stepfather must have found it. Next thing I know the police raided the house, and I got arrested. He told them I was incorrigible. I did eight months in juvenile hall and was a ward of the court from then on."

In the later part of the 1960s, criminal street gangs, such as the Crips and the Bloods, were just getting started. A phenomenon originating in the city of Los Angeles, it soon invaded virtually every urban neighborhood in the nation. So much so a study published by National Youth Gang Survey of Law Enforcement Agencies in 2002 published by the Office of Juvenile Justice and Delinquency Prevention estimated there were roughly 26,000 different criminal street gangs boasting

731,500 total members in the United States.[3] These statistics remained roughly the same through the end of 2019.

The insidious methodology of street gangs is not only the claiming of a certain turf or 'hood, but the segregated neighborhoods encouraged racial violence. This wasn't always the case out on the street, but once gang members got sentenced to jail, prison, or juvenile hall, inmates segregated themselves by race. Each racial group—predominantly Blacks, Hispanics, and Whites—sought dominance over the others. Sadly, as the rest of the nation strove to become more integrated, our jails, prisons, and juvenile halls became hot beds of racism and gang-style violence. At the age of sixteen Michael Lee had to defend himself in one of the first schools to teach gangsterism, Los Angeles County juvenile hall.

Michael knew how to take care of himself, he knew when he was challenged, he better not back down. "I just went crazy on the other guy." The one thing his stepfather taught him was how to take a punch. "I could take a lickin', and keep on tickin.'" It didn't take long for Michael to earn some "respect," particularly because he stood up for the "little guys," the kids being bullied by older wards.

The eight months passed slowly for Michael, but it wasn't all bad. Once he got the rules down and established a reputation, the structure of the hall had real advantages. Michael had to go to school, and there weren't any drugs around, so in many ways he prospered. The chaos of his homelife, and the random acts of violence he suffered, made the hall safe by comparison. At least if he had to fight, it would be a fair fight. A couple months before his scheduled release, the staff recognized Michael's progress: "they made me president of the hall."

Then he was released back into the environment that got him arrested in the first place. Things at home were worse than ever. His mother and stepfather had split up. Michael soon learned it was because his mother was having sex with some of his friends who came around looking for him.

"That really weirded me out, I just couldn't live at home anymore. So, I left, but this time nobody cared I was gone. That's the second time I was homeless, at sixteen. I had a vacant trailer I could sleep in for a while, but most of the time I just found a spot on the beach."

Survival wasn't easy for a homeless sixteen-year-old. Just eating was a daily struggle. "I collected bottles and cans, and I got lucky, I found a market that would leave stale food out for me."

At eighteen Michael's uncle in Oklahoma finally tracked him down. "He gave me a job working on his ranch. I stayed there, so I could keep my money. Finally saved enough to buy a car and drive back to Redondo; that was a big mistake. I moved in with some old friends, you know, the guys I used to party with—it went downhill from there."

His uncle taught him the benefits of hard work, so Michael could pay his share of the rent and cover the cost of his growing addiction. Then he got arrested as an adult, for possession of barbiturates. His stay in L.A. County was short. "I got appointed a real good lawyer, he questioned the probable cause to search me, got the case dismissed."

"Eventually, I got a job on the line for an aerospace company, and no matter what I did the night before, I managed to show up to work on time." Michael became one of the millions of functioning addicts and/or alcoholics who manage to hold down a job. Survival remains a priority, but the addiction eventually takes over. "Some people last longer than others, but they all 'crash and burn' sooner or later."

Partying every night and working most days didn't keep Michael from falling in love. "I met a beautiful girl, she liked to party, but she kept it under control. We got married, had two kids, that's when she got it together. I thought I had it under control. I loved my family, but I didn't stop. I tried to hide it. It went along like that alright until I met the 'meth monster.'"

Methamphetamine swept through the nation in the 1980s as a cheaper, synthetic substitute for cocaine. A powerful stimulant, the euphoria lasts for hours. Amphetamines were first sold by prescription as "diet pills." Taken off the market after tens of thousands got addicted, low doses of it were still used in daytime cold remedies. Formulas for extracting the drug from over-the-counter pills allowed for the creation of "meth labs." Addicts could create their own methamphetamine and sell the rest on the streets. Eventually, laws were passed removing the precursor for methamphetamine from cold remedies, but the genie was out of the bottle. The cartels got hold of the formula and set up meth labs across the border. More potent and cheaper to make than cocaine, and more addictive, methamphetamine quickly replaced cocaine as our nation's most popular street drug.

Witnessing the ravages of methamphetamine addiction has been one of the great sorrows of my life. Other drugs are highly addictive, but no other substance so fundamentally alters the basic character and personality of a long-term user. As an "upper" it makes the user more aggressive, and the euphoria is diabolical. It is chemically induced psychopathy, granting its user the ability to lie, cheat, and steal with impunity. Suppressing the conscience, it leaves behind a narcissistic addict perpetually in search of his next high. Worst of all is the withering pain experienced when brain synapses are no longer stimulated by the drug. Avoiding the terror of withdrawal becomes the user's sole purpose in life.

"She finally left me. She took the kids, gave me a big kiss that morning, I came home and everything and everybody was gone. That sent me over the edge, all I had left was the drug. I couldn't get into work anymore; to get rid of the pain, I used more, I think that's when I started injecting it."

Michael fell back into the streets and this time he fell harder. He had a punishing drug habit to finance. "I wound up in the San Fernando Valley living behind buildings, vacant lots, anywhere I could get away with sleeping in a cardboard condo. I lived like that for a long time, till I was forty-three years old."

Michael's grandmother finally came to the rescue. She managed to find him and send him a plane ticket to Oklahoma. "She still loved me, and I was at the end of my rope. I left all my connections behind, she nursed me through the hell of it all, and I took care of her after that, she was getting pretty old. I managed to keep it together when I lived with her. I stayed sober for three years.

"When she died, it sent me over the edge, I went out and bought a big bag of dope, started right up again."

His first brush with the law in Oklahoma was for a joint of marijuana, a felony for which he got probation. He was now on law enforcement's radar, so when his name was offered up by a snitch, they knew who they were looking for. "I had an eighth of an ounce of meth hidden in my gas tank. It makes you paranoid, the more you use it; so, I started carrying a gun. I had a nine-millimeter in the car, so, when I drove into a road block, I never had a chance. They pulled me out of the car, took me to the ground, handcuffed, boot on my face, I watched them go right to it. Opened the gas tank, pulled out the dope, tore up my car, found the gun on the front seat."

Michael bailed out and got a lawyer. Possession of drugs with a gun while on probation, he was looking at five years in prison. "It didn't matter, as soon as I got out, I started right up again."

Michael decided it was time to go to the source, so he made a trip over the border. "I went to South Padre Island, coming back I put the dope up under the hood, where there was a lot of grease and oil, dogs can't smell it there." He made it over the border but when he got home the place was torn apart and everything of value was gone. "I let some young guys stay there, they were growing pot in the backyard, when the cops showed up, they said the plants were mine. They put a warrant out for my arrest."

Michael got his shotgun and went looking for his former tenants. When he caught up to them, seeing the gun, "they really freaked out. Instead of giving me my stuff back they called the cops. Driving away I chucked the gun into a field, when they pulled me over, I said I never had a gun. They let me go, but they went back and found the gun."

Michael now had two warrants for his arrest, one for cultivation, the other for assault with a firearm, and a probation violation on his drug conviction. "I was desperate, I knew it was just a matter of time before they caught up with me. I wasn't gettin' out this time; I knew I'd be sent up state."

Michael carried a necklace with a small wooden cross on it, he hung it from his rearview mirror. The terror of his current circumstances, enhanced by the pain of withdrawal, overtook him. "That's when I reached up and grabbed that cross in my hands and prayed: 'Father God, lead me somewhere else; where I can help myself and others.'

"God answered my prayers because that's when I got arrested. I crossed into Texas with dope under the hood and seven grand in my pocket. A police dog hit on my truck and they tore it apart until they found it. Some 'good old boy' Texas Ranger sat me down and told me if I donated the money to the police league, they wouldn't charge me. I took the deal, but he didn't let me go, they took me back to Oklahoma."

When Michael got to court his lawyer told him he was looking at thirty years. He got him a deal for ten, but the assault with a deadly weapon charge was a "violent felony" requiring him to serve eighty-five percent of his time—Michael would have to serve at least eight and a half years.

Convicted of a violent crime, Michael was sent to Cimarron, a high-security prison. "It was all ganged up, Hispanic gangs, Crips, Bloods, and United Aryan Brotherhood (UAB), they ran the place. I tried to stay out of it, but they get around to everybody sooner or later. I was walking the line below, and I looked up and saw some Crips smokin' crack in their cell, and they saw me. Next day two of 'em beat me to a pulp. Wanted to make sure I wouldn't snitch 'em off.

"I spent some time in the infirmary, doctor took a look at me because I was pretty beat up. The good news was I would recover from my injuries, but only if I lived long enough. He told me I had an enlarged heart from all the meth: 'You probably won't last ninety days.' I knew it was true, my legs were so swollen, I could feel my heart failing. Somehow I got better though; prayer saved my life."

In virtually every prison in the United States there are Christians who regularly visit and disciple prisoners. Prison Fellowship and Awana Lifeline are national ministries providing moral and spiritual training to inmates, but there are also countless local ministries and individuals who bring the gospel of Jesus Christ behind prison walls. But for the saints living out Christ's command in Matthew 25:32–46 to provide for "the least of these" by visiting the prisoner the same as "you did it for me," prisoners might be denied the cure for the disease that ails them.

Our forefathers understood this as the root of the term "penitentiary" comes from the Christian discipline of doing "penitence." Penitence being "the state of having regret for doing something wrong." Disastrously, Supreme Court decisions on the First Amendment's alleged "separation of church and state" have caused wardens to exclude religious moral training from any inmate services. This policy is largely responsible for recidivism rates hovering around 60 percent. Societal frustration with this failure and the resulting violent crime rates have led to decades of "tough on crime" laws and a criminal justice system based on retribution.[4]

However, the situation is far from hopeless, as the saints doing prison ministry and their converts will tell you. One of those converts is Michael Lee. "There was one man—Tom was his name—he was a very successful business man, 'the millionaire' we called him. He came to Cimarron every week to lead a Bible study. All the Christian guys went to his Bible study, and church on Sunday. With everything going on in my life, I fell in with them. When the UAB came around and wanted to know what I wanted to do about those black guys beating me up, I told 'em nothing. I said, 'I've already forgiven them.' They were amazed. I think I might have stopped a race riot telling them that."

The one place racial segregation is not enforced by prison gangs is where Christians meet. Church on Sunday in prison is perhaps the most integrated service in the nation. "Even the worst of the worst have a right to save their own soul." This gangster ethic is what allows sincere Christians to break down the racism enforced everywhere else in prison.

I have been blessed to be a parishioner in many a prison church, and I can tell you there is no joy quite like singing "Amazing Grace" with two or three hundred prisoners. Best of all is a baptism. As mentioned earlier, there are no baptismals, so creative alternatives—usually a trash bin filled to the brim with water—serves the purpose. This is how Michael was baptized.

"When I got baptized, it was awesome. I truly felt 'born again.' Everyone was clapping and rejoicing . . . still brings tears to my eyes. I promised God right then, no more drugs, alcohol, smoking—nothing."

Michael did his time, and it would be dishonest to say it was easy. The dangers and temptations of prison life still came looking for him, but he kept his promise to God. "One time I came back to my cell, and my cellie had an ounce of cocaine laid out on his desk. He told me, 'Take whatever you want,' but something in me had changed. I looked at that mountain of dope and it just disgusted me. I wanted nothing to do with it."

Finally, the day came, after nine years Michael was released. He managed to save nine hundred dollars working inside the prison. When he first started, he got paid fifteen dollars a month. Due to cuts in Oklahoma's Corrections budget, he was making five dollars a month at the end. "When I got out, they gave me a check for $900 and a bus ticket to Los Angeles."

Nine hundred dollars isn't much anywhere, but in Los Angeles it's not even first month's rent. About 25 percent of all parolees join the ranks of the homeless. No education, no job training, and being a convicted felon is hard to overcome when you're looking for a job. Being in his early sixties didn't help either. Michael no longer did drugs or engaged in a criminal lifestyle, but he struggled to find a place to live. "I stayed in my cousin's backyard, he had a tiny trailer I could use when it rained, but a lot of the time I just slept on the ground. I used his hose to 'shower,' wash clothes, that sort of thing."

This time Michael didn't let his circumstances bring him down. He had a new mission in life. "I decided I wanted to help others like me. I made daily excursions into homeless camps, bringing them food, personal items, that sort of thing. One of the places I'd go was Harbor Memorial Hospital in Torrance. A lot of homeless folks were coming in and out of there, so it was a place where I could help out. That's where I met Miriam."

Miriam Rounds enjoyed a long and successful career in the corporate world, but then the recession of 2008 hit, and she was laid off. Rather than grieve her own misfortune, Miriam decided to spend her time helping others worse off than herself. She got involved with Harbor Interfaith, a non-profit working with local city and county agencies to find housing for the homeless.

Working together, Miriam and Michael became friends. Learning of Michael's conversion, she invited him to go to church with her. "I had some bad experiences with church people when I was a kid; I didn't want to go, but Miriam stayed on me about it so I showed up on Sunday. That's when I met Pastor Pete. I told him I didn't think I'd be back 'cause of my issues. He said, 'Well, let's talk about that.'

"I thought I could escape by saying I might come by some-time, but instead he said, 'Let's talk right now.' He got my whole life story and before long he was asking me if I'd give my testimony at church. It made me real nervous, but I did it."

Miriam kept after Michael about finding permanent housing. "I told her I was doing fine; she should take care of someone who needed it more than me. She wore me down though; eventually I agreed to an apartment I could afford in a subsidized housing complex. Most everyone living there had been homeless. It was a madhouse—needles in the hallway, people partying all night long. The guy in the room next to me would play his electric guitar 'til three or four in the morning. I couldn't sleep, so I finally took a box of food over to him and told him, 'I've never called the police on no one, but this has got to stop.' He took the food and things got better with him, but I couldn't live there—not and stay sober.

"Then the Lord really smiled on me; I found a little house in Lomita that took subsidized housing. I can't believe how nice it is, and how happy I am now. I had no idea life could be this good."

Having represented countless drug addicts and alcoholics in my time, what still amazes me is the ability of the human body, mind, and spirit to recover once sobriety is achieved. Michael's calm demeanor, capable intellect, and caring spirit are a prime example. His addiction ran rampant for almost forty years causing all of the usual destruction. Yet, if you were to meet him for the first time today, you would never suspect the pain of his past. He retains some of the physical scars of the car accident, and his liver is permanently damaged, but he is of sound mind and joyful spirit. What is still more amazing, even miraculous, Michael carries no grudges, and he has no regrets. "If I had it to do over again, I wouldn't change a thing. This is how I met Jesus, and that's sacred. All I want to do now is help others get to where I am."

This is the last thing Michael tells me before his attention is drawn to the opening of the fellowship hall doors. His mission in life comes into focus as they enter the room in polite appreciation. They are a diverse cross section of the community—old, young, and in-between—men and women of every racial mix. Most everyone is dressed in the casual attire of a beach community, having left their worldly possessions at the door you wouldn't know they are living on the streets. A few stand out as more at-risk than others, an elderly man in a wheelchair, a woman wearing a floor-length coat who stands apart quietly muttering to herself, and a young man with long, sun-bleached hair and scraggly beard, who displays the agitated demeanor of someone under the influence. All in all, though, there is a sense of community, they know each other, many are friends, and they are happy to be here.

I sit with Michael at a table stacked with mail in a far corner of the room. A line forms, Michael checks in with each of his charges before letting them move on. Next to us Deacon Kathy Pinkerton assists with applications for government housing. She patiently interviews the applicant and fills it out in perfect handwriting.

From across the room, I hear greeting calls of "Pastor Pete." In his early thirties, Pastor Pete looks too young to be the "senior" pastor of Saint Andrew's. However, standing six foot three with light brown hair and clear blue eyes, his physical stature nicely compensates for his youthful appearance. He smiles broadly, enjoying the enthusiastic welcome. When he speaks, his voice carries throughout the room; he has mastered the skill of projection. I see Michael wink at me out of the corner of his eye.

"The devotional today comes from Psalms 123 and 124. 'Have mercy on us, O LORD, have mercy on us, for we have endured no end of contempt. We have endured no end of ridicule from the arrogant, of contempt from the proud.'"

As he preaches, I lean back in my chair to discreetly wipe the moisture from my eyes. I tell myself it's his passion for the downtrodden that touches me so, but of course it's more than that; perhaps I am a little too proud.

He continues, "Praise be to the LORD . . . we have escaped like a bird from the fowler's snare; the snare has been broken, and we have escaped. Our help is in the name of the LORD, the Maker of heaven and earth." A strong "amen" is offered by the parishioners of what Pastor Pete calls his second church.

"Alright, I'll say a blessing for the food and then we'll get started."

As he says grace, I open my eyes to check on his congregation, I see no one who has not bowed his head or clasped her hands in prayer. It seems almost surreal to me. I can hardly believe the preacher saying the prayer is my son, the Reverend Peter Remington Dunn.

Michael smiles at me warmly and picks up a large stack of envelopes. He will spend the next hour making his rounds delivering the mail and helping out others less fortunate than himself.

Baja Bob

The sun was almost straight over head in El Florito, Mexico. Fortunately, it rarely gets hot here; rather we almost always enjoy the moderating influence of an ocean breeze. Twenty miles inland from the Pacific, Rosarita Beach to be exact, the low rolling hills allow the ocean air to move in at night, slowly burning away as the day grows longer. If we were to travel thirty miles north as the crow flies, we would land in some of the most high-end real estate in the United States. These same hills provide for miles and miles of cliffs overlooking sandy beaches with the same comfort of a Mediterranean climate. Luxury homes and hi-tech businesses cover the landscape making San Diego County one of the most desirable places to live in the nation.

But the only thing El Florito has in common with San Diego is the topography and the climate. Yes, all kinds of people live on the hillsides and in the valleys below, but most of them are desperately poor. Shacks and lean-to structures provide most of the housing, erected on small pads carved out of the hillsides by the government. The deal is if a family can build a "house," some sort of structure with a roof overhead, and pay the equivalent of fifty dollars a month, they can stay. No plumbing, but if they can throw a wire over the power lines, they have electricity.

I'd been coming here about twice a year for over thirty years. Much has changed as the coming of NAFTA caused assembly plants for electronics and some car manufacturers to be built all along the border. Many improvements have been made, new roads to accommodate trucks heading for the border, and the development of commercial shopping centers to provide for the ever-growing population. This would seem to be a good thing, and it is for some, but for most of the workers in the factories the prevailing wage of a dollar an hour is barely subsistence living. Enough to pay the government its fifty dollars, buy food and water to survive, and maybe some used clothing now and then. A real home to live in remains out of reach for most people.

So, we build them a house. When I say *we*, I mean Baja Christian Ministries and whatever church or other group of do-gooders who can raise $8,500 and dare to cross the border to spend a weekend building it. A little "A" frame on a cement slab, about twenty feet square. Two bedrooms, a living area, with an upstairs loft for the kids. Shingle roof, plywood exterior, drywall interior, three windows with screens, and a front door including door knob with lock and keys. Wired for electricity on the inside, painted any color of the rainbow on the outside, the bright colors of our houses can be spotted throughout the valley and up into the hillsides.

It wasn't this easy in the beginning, and we sure couldn't get a house done in a weekend. We had a slab to work on, but we had to cut all the lumber ourselves. Now, the wood is all pre-cut to the specific dimensions of the house so the walls and rafters fit together like an erector set. Nail guns and drills for drywall screws make it possible to get it done in as little as ten hours. So, when our church, Malibu Presbyterian, left Malibu at 6:00 a.m. on a Saturday, we could be home by 9:00 p.m. on Sunday, spending one night at the La Especial Hotel in Tecate. We spend more time driving and sitting at the border than building the house.

For me this has to be right around a hundred structures built. Not all of them were houses; we doubled up the size of the structure sometimes so it could be used as a church, orphanage, or in one case the local police station. My favorite was a chapel we built inside Ensenada Prison.

The current house was almost done. The youngsters were on the roof finishing up, I worked inside on the last of the drywall. I'm still amazed that with all these houses I've worked on, how little I've learned about carpentry. I do my best work as a laborer carrying lumber, shingles, and drywall, thus avoiding bending another nail. On the second day of construction, I was spent. Time for a water break.

≪ ≪ ≫ ≫

Finding a place in the shade, I had a chance to reflect on how it all started. A friend of mine—no, more than that—a personal mentor, Paul Shoop, asked me if I wanted to go to Mexico with him. Paul was from Texas and looked and acted his heritage wherever he went. Paul was also a lawyer, about fifteen years older than me, and when I started out in private practice, he took me under his wing. He referred me cases and showed me how to run a business. He helped this young lawyer make a go of it. So, when Paul told me he'd bought an old drilling rig in Texas, and had it shipped over the border so he could drill water wells in a place called El Florito, I couldn't tell him I didn't want to go to see it with him.

The plan was to meet "Baja Bob" at 10:00 a.m., just this side of the Tijuana border. I was expecting another cowboy, but Bob Sanders was anything but—rather he might just be the softest spoken and humblest a man I've ever met. About 5'10", prematurely gray, thin build, and not speaking a word of Spanish, he didn't fit my expectation of a guide through Mexico. Worse, the car we were traveling in was an ancient VW Bus that backfired often. Paul wasn't the least bit concerned, so I hid my anxiety as best I could.

I soon found out being a missionary to Mexico was a new gig for Bob. He took a trip over the border with a group from Azusa Pacific University where he worked as a janitor. So moved by the abject poverty and the lack of fresh drinking water, Bob asked the university for a small grant to help the poorest of the poor in Mexico. Somehow, he got together with Paul, who was now underwriting what would soon become Baja Christian Ministries.

Crossing the border further raised my anxiety level. Stoplights were soon replaced by red "Alto" signs, despite the intense city traffic. The road deteriorated quickly, and lanes of travel merged into one large flowing stream. It looked like chaos, until I noticed the level of cooperation among the drivers. They drove with patience and courtesy for one another, compensating for the lack of formal regulation. About ten miles in, we switched from pavement to dirt. The ride got rougher, but we still moved at a good clip because most of the ruts were worn away since it was so well traveled.

The farther south we went, the more it became clear we were in a third-world country. The commercial buildings along the border, and the brick and stucco houses, gave way to the wooden shacks of Mexico's interior. Thousands upon thousands of small shelters dotted the hillsides, only broken apart by the dirt roads connecting them. Trash of every type lined the "highway" we were traveling, further blighting what was recently the green rolling hillsides of spring. The worst of it was the smell. Black smoke of trash fires spread a lingering stench across the valley floor. With no place to take their garbage, the people have no other way of disposing of their accumulated waste.

None of this seemed to bother our guide. Bob drove along happily describing each community, the people living there, where they worked, where they came from, that sort of thing. Our pace continued to slow as the farther south we went the rougher the roads became.

"We're coming into El Florito now, this is the poorest community I've seen. Most of the people here are migrants from the south of Mexico, or even Guatemala," Bob explained. "Some of them don't even speak Spanish, just their native languages."

"Why do they come?" Paul asked.

"Poverty, of course, but also political violence. The people of Central America are still caught in the middle of a communist insurgency and the repressive governments battling with them. It's in this community as well, some of the homes have a hammer and sickle painted on their doors. We put crosses on the homes we build, and our goal is to replace all those hammers and sickles with crosses."

As we approached our destination, we passed some women and children carrying large plastic jugs of water. "I'll bet they got that from our well," Bob buoyantly said. "They'll walk for miles to get fresh water, especially if it's free." Our pace slowed to a walk as too many people jammed the roadway. Finally, we pulled up next to a group of locals standing in a circle, waiting their turn as water from a steel pipe poured out onto the ground. The strong spring spewed forth a fountain of fresh water. The locals held out bottles trying to capture as much they can, as their children played beneath them in a newly created water park. Joy filled the air, a spontaneous festival broke out, a celebration observing the life-sustaining character of fresh water. Paul walked to the drilling rig parked nearby. The crew was taking a break, letting the people enjoy the moment before capping the well. Paul's pride was evident as he put out his hand to each man, saying, "*Gracias, Señor.*"

Losing track of time in the moment, mid-afternoon crept up on us—a concern, as we decided earlier we needed to get back to the border before dark. Navigating the hinterland of Mexico was not what we wanted to do at night. I timed our route from the border at just under two hours and assumed the same going back, so I thought we would be alright. Bob agreed, and we got back on the road.

After about an hour I noticed we had turned onto "Highway 2 to Tecate." Bob explained, "We're going to cross at Otay Mesa; the line isn't nearly as long as Tijuana."

"Sounds good to me." I was ready to get back to American soil.

Traveling east did nothing to improve the roads, but at long last we came to a fork in the road and turned left heading for the border. Suddenly, our transportation started to sputter and then just as quickly stopped altogether. We coasted a short distance then pulled to the side of the road.

"Sorry, it's been having a fuel line problem, I know how to fix it," Bob assured us.

Paul remained unflappable, but I barely kept my anger in check. Dusk was upon us and we were in the middle of nowhere. No cars, no buildings, and no people. The only structure I saw was as ominous as it gets: a prison under construction loomed down upon us from a hillside about three hundred yards above the road. The observation towers at each corner of the reinforced concrete made it unmistakable.

Bob got out and opened the back of the bus where the four-banger sat tucked between the back wheels. Paul got out to help; I reluctantly followed.

Pulling a clear tube from what I figured must be the carburetor, Bob sucked on it until it was filled with gasoline. He spit on the ground, two or three times before rehooking the tube, and asked, "Phil, can you get me that bottle of water in the back seat?"

"You bet." I opened the sliding door and handed the bottle to Bob who took a swig and spit it out.

"Okay, Paul, why don't you give it a try." With a twist of the ignition key, the engine turned over, but it didn't start. Bob looked perplexed; Paul for the first time looked concerned.

"Wow, that's always worked before . . ."

"Worked before?" I grumbled.

"Well, let's give it another try; it's definitely not getting any gas." Paul preferred to be helpful; I began contemplating worse-case scenarios. *Can we walk to the border from here? Is it safe? Maybe hitchhike?*

Bob repeated the same process, spitting out enough gas so the smell of it permeated the air. I was already feeling nauseous, raw gasoline fumes wasn't helping my condition.

The labored whine of an electric starter played on and on as Paul provided rhythm by pumping the gas pedal. Nothing—not so much as a spark. "That's enough, I don't want to wear down the battery," Paul conceded.

Great . . . dead battery, that ought to do us in.

Bob opened the back again, and fiddled with some more hoses, but it was obvious he didn't know what was wrong. Panic entered my consciousness, but I suppressed the emotion knowing it would just make things worse. Instead, I let my attention drift back to the prison in the distance. With the advent of dusk, a low-level fog rolled in. The gray prison walls were being touched by approaching fingers of fog accelerating the coming on of darkness. This surreal scene reminded me of Tolkien's description of the gates outside Mordor.

Then, beneath the walls, I saw something move. A moat of sorts surrounded the prison—somewhere in the dirt excavated to buttress the foundation of the walls. Within the moat, massive amounts of trash had been dumped, as if it were a landfill. A haze of black smoke lingered just above the moat coming from the small fires still smoldering within.

I saw more movement—people—their heads visible just above the crest of the ridge. I started walking, drawn to the scene as if I'm catching a glimpse of the Apocalypse. As I got closer, I saw they were women and children rummaging through the trash. The women carried large bags on their shoulders, some had sifters, others carefully picked through the trash with their bare hands as the children played with whatever they could find within the pit.

Stopping just outside the moat, I stood and watched with a mix of sorrow and amazement. Hearing footsteps, I turned to see Paul had followed me. His bold demeanor melted into one of obvious sadness. We watched in silence, mesmerized by an unimaginable scene of destitute poverty. I wanted to help—to do something, anything—but they were too many. Despair came over me as I realized there was nothing to be done.

Paul finally spoke: "I think we were meant to see this."

"Yes, it's no coincidence we stopped here."

These were the only words spoken between us as we lingered there. Finally, we turned away and walked back to the bus in silence. The scene needed to be processed.

Back at the bus, Bob did nothing to elevate our mood: "I don't know what else to do, I've tried everything I can think of."

I was angry—anger born of fear. *How could he have brought us into Mexico in a beat-up bus he knew had problems?*

"Let's give it one more try." Paul refused to join me in blaming Bob. Paul tried the engine again, but still nothing. Worse, it was slowing down—the battery was about dead.

"Suggestions, gentlemen?" Paul remained calm despite what I believed to be a hopeless situation. Having nothing to offer, I remained silent.

"Well, the only thing I can think of is we lay hands on the engine," replied Bob.

I looked Bob in the eyes and realized he was serious . . . my astonishment was obvious. Paul smiled, revealing the courage of someone who enjoyed a little danger now and then.

"We've been here over an hour now, the engine should have cooled down, shouldn't be a problem." Bob's concern for our safety didn't impress me.

"We got nothing to lose—alright, Bob, you start and I'll finish." Paul went to his knees and opened the hood, and reached for the engine. Bob got down on the other side, leaving me a spot in the middle. Going to my knees, I grabbed the top of the cylinders and closed my eyes. Bob started with a plea for "divine intervention," I begged for "help and protection," and Paul finished with a few specifics about "gasoline and spark plugs." We concluded with a powerful, "Amen."

"Okay, Bob, you give it a try." Paul was still smiling.

Bob sat in the driver's seat, closed his eyes, and dropped his head to the steering wheel. We waited for him to finish another silent prayer, then he turned the key. *Varoom*, it started! Elation filled our ranks—the joy of rescue, our own little personal miracle.

Bob hit the gas, the four-banger engine answered with enthusiasm, and I did a little victory dance before high-fiving Paul.

Bob went from goat to hero in an instant. This humble janitor from Azusa obviously had some sort of connection.

I remembered little about the drive to the border, or how long it took to get home that night. Eventually the joy dissipated, and alternative explanations for our salvation were considered. After much discussion, we abandoned our rational minds; it was just too perfect. Not just the prayer for rescue, but where we were stopped.

Paul and I often discussed the women and children of the prison moat, and why we were meant to see them. The message was strong but not specific. So powerful was the image, it returned to me one night in a dream. My heart was broken and I could feel the tears running down my cheeks. When I awoke, these words entered my mind: "If you do nothing, this is the way it will be."

Paul also embraced this sentiment, and so, we devised a plan on to support Baja Bob Sanders and his ministry to the poor of Mexico. It hasn't always been easy, ministry on a shoestring never is, but Bob persevered.

≪ ≪ ≫ ≫

A few more bangs from the nail gun brought me back to the present. The last of the shingles were being nailed into the final corner of the roof and the front door was hung. It was time to present the keys to the freshly hung front door. This is an honor I reserve for myself, choosing the members of our crew who present the keys to the family.

Our family this time is particularly beautiful. Mom and Dad have to be in their early twenties, grandparents—on her side, I think—and three little girls, ages six, four, and two. The two-year-old stayed close to her mother, but the other two charmed us by doing their best to help. I directed them to the ladies painting trim—their hands and faces were spotted yellow and blue, the colors of their new home.

Bob arrived in a weather-beaten pickup truck, with three mattresses in the back. A new bed for each of the homes we have built.

"Phil Dunn, so good to see you, brother." Bob always draws unwanted attention to me; I've gotten used to it. "Good to see you, Bob."

I picked up one end of a mattress with a younger, stronger fellow, and walked it down the hill to the house. Four of us then pushed it up into the loft. Bob wasn't finished: "We had enough money to buy some pillows and comforters, and even a few stuffed animals."

A couple of the ladies from our painting crew knew just what to do. Gathering the two eldest girls, they walked them up the stairs and taught them how to fit sheets to mattress. They had them lie down next to each other, placing a pillow under each of their heads and then spreading the comforter over them. The final touch, a couple of long-eared stuffed puppies. Friends to sleep with in the first bed of their own. Giggles from the girls, and sniffles from the ladies filled the room.

Our crew included a group of teenagers from Malibu High School and their parents. The trip provided a healthy dose of culture shock for any first-timers, residents of Malibu in particular. I watched as two Malibu moms descended the stairs and upon safely reaching the floor, one turned to me, and asked, "Who does this?"

"You do this."

I received a small nod of recognition as she wiped away tears. I handed her the key to the front door. "We're about to start the key ceremony, so why don't you say a little something before giving them the key."

"What do I say?"

"Whatever comes to you in the moment will be just fine."

Bob called from outside, "Come on everyone, let's gather round the family, and say a few words." As everyone congregated around the front of the house, Bob started telling the "Starfish Story." Bob always tells this story—I've heard it a hundred times, but his enthusiasm for its message never changes.

"It was low tide at the beach on a very hot day, and everywhere attached to the rocks were starfish, baking in the sun. A boy walks onto the beach, and realizing the starfish are dying, he begins picking them off the rocks and throwing them back out into the ocean. An old man walks over to the boy. 'Little boy, don't you realize that there are thousands of starfish dying on this beach—you can't save them all, you'll never make a difference.' The boy stops for a moment to consider the old man's words, and then picks up another starfish and throws it into the ocean saying, 'It made a difference to that one.'"

Bob lets the story sink in a little before saying, "Brother Phil, will you lead us in a word of prayer as we lay hands on the family?"

I had long since overcome my discomfort with the laying on of hands. My prayer was typically short—it is for the family, especially the children, and all the other "starfish" in the neighborhood.

Three of the team came forward to hand Mr. and Mrs. Ibarra the keys to their new home. Through an interpreter he thanked us, and then said, "Please know that I, my family, all of us will never forget this and we will always lift all of you up in our prayers."

Soon we were loaded into our late-model trucks and SUVs. Leaving the neighborhood, we passed a homeless encampment. Like our own country, these were the poorest of the poor, except here there were no government services. Most of them were recent immigrants who traveled as far north as they could. The best of their shelters were lean-tos, oftentimes made from garage doors imported from the United States. Most were in poorly fashioned tents; many had no shelter at all. I was reminded of the women and children of the moat, and the cynical old man in me reared his ugly head. Three decades later, and the life of the poor in Mexico is probably worse than when we started.

Then, I caught myself and remembered the words of Mother Teresa. When she was awarded the Nobel Peace Prize, the secular press descended upon her. One particularly cynical reporter asked, "Can you tell me if it's any better now than when you first started working with the poor of Calcutta."

"No," she answered, "if anything it is worse now than when we started."

Then came the gotcha question, "So what's the point, why do you bother, if you're not making a difference?"

"Because God does not call us to be successful—just faithful."

Epilogue

There are no ordinary people. You have never talked to a mere mortal. Nations, cultures, arts, civilizations—these are mortal, and their life is to ours as the life of a gnat. —C. S. Lewis

E ach of us has an immortal soul. Even the universe will end someday, but you and I are so loved by God, our spirits have no end. This truth is self-evident in the life stories of Santana Acuna, Rico Ramirez, Andrew Tahmooressi, Michael Lee, Bob Sanders, Jorge Garcia, and John Jenks. God intervened in their lives. The results may differ, but the love revealed to them was manifest.

Santana Acuna started Special Forces Discipleship Church—a ministry dedicated to keeping the youth of the Inland Empire out of criminal street gangs. As a respected member in the 'hood, Santana's conversion became a powerful testimony heard on the streets and in churches throughout the community.

Having represented hundreds of gang members in my time, it has been my experience the most effective response to the violence caused by the proliferation of criminal street gangs comes with local ministries such as Special Forces Discipleship. Similar to addiction, the grip that gangster life holds over young men and women requires a spiritual power greater than the evil holding them. We Christians know this "higher power" to be the God of the Bible. It is impossible to know just how many souls Santana lured away from the misery of his past. No one had a better platform to speak the truth in love.

I had lunch with Santana a few years ago. He still retained all the trappings of a serious gangster. Only when he spoke of his ministry did his demeanor soften; he obviously took pride in its success. He was in his seventies at the time, and all of the abuse his body endured in his youth had taken its toll. It was about a year later when I received a call from his wife, telling me, "Pastor Santana has gone on to be with the Lord."

Rico Ramirez did a year at the Victory Outreach Men's Home and thereafter successfully completed his probation. He went through their discipleship program, and then they sent him to the south of Chicago as a missionary. At the time, and to this day, South Chicago is the most violent neighborhood in America. Gang warfare over control of the drug trade has given Chicago the title "homicide capitol of the nation," due to a murder rate of over 700 per year.

Rico was fearless in his evangelism, often giving his testimony on street corners with a blow horn. Rico's passion has always been saving gang members. He sought out the leadership of rival gangs in an effort to negotiate a truce. His efforts were recognized by the Chicago Police Department who issued him a police identification card making it possible for him to visit inmates in the Cook County Jail.

"Did you ever think, Phil, that I'd be working with 'the man'?" Rico asked me as he took out his wallet to show me the card. "No, Rico, I didn't see that one coming."

Unfortunately, Rico, like Santana, carried the afflictions of his past—in his case, hepatitis that caused major liver damage. His brother, Pastor Eddy Ramirez, let me know of Rico's passing recently. Maria Ramirez has greatly mourned the loss of her oldest son, but it has not slowed her down. She still runs a Bible study in the Ventura County Jail every week for Spanish-speaking inmates.

Andrew Tahmooressi also retains scars of the trauma he endured. He had PTSD before he went into prison in Mexico, and he will tell you what he experienced there was worse than his combat tours in Afghanistan. Andrew has made the best of it all, though the road he has traveled has been bumpy at times. Jill remains a good friend and as faithful as ever. She continues to work as a nursing supervisor with no immediate plan for retirement. Andrew and Jill often attend the Church by the Glades describing themselves as "rock solid Christians." Jill in particular appreciates her return to normal life and the peace of mind her faith has given her.

Michael Lee continues to deliver the mail, though the risk to his health is greater than ever due to COVID-19. Pastor Pete let him know he didn't have to make the rounds of the homeless encampments anymore, but Michael would hear none of that. His work load doubled, as Michael took on the task of delivering food baskets and masks to everyone he ministers to. "I still have a lot of pain, and my liver is just barely hanging in there, but I'm not going to let it slow me down. It may take me six days a week now, but I still get to everyone on my route."

Baja Bob Sanders turned the day-to-day operations of Baja Christian Ministries over to his son-in-law Eric Prager a few years ago. Eric's commitment and energy have helped make the program flourish. We have now built over 2,500 hundred homes on the Baja Peninsula, along with an assortment of churches, orphanages, school houses, drug rehabilitation centers, and even one local police station. The discipleship teaching known as the "Purple Book," has had over 600,000 people complete the program. It is taught in almost every prison in Mexico, and I have seen whole sections of the prison yard set aside for classes and worship services numbering in the hundreds.

During one trip to Mexico, we built a chapel inside Ensenada Prison. Rico Ramirez came with me that time, and I will always remember his wonderment about being allowed to carry a hammer and a dry wall knife inside a prison. He told me, "Phil, you don't know what it means to me to be able to walk into a prison, and then at the end of the day walk right out."

Jorge Garcia remains a dear friend and committed soldier for Christ. Some of his work with Prison Fellowship has been affected by COVID-19, as civilians are no longer allowed inside prisons in the United States. Jorge recently was diagnosed with cancer, and the treatment slowed him down for a while, but he has made a complete recovery, and no one is stopping him from going into prisons in Mexico, Central America, and South America. He recently asked me, "Phil, I'm going to Columbia next month, why don't you come along with me."

"Jorge, that's just a bridge too far for me." Instead, we made plans to go to Ensenada to check on the chapel we built.

Len finally retired, so John Jenks does all my investigations along with rehabilitation counseling. John also bears the wounds of his previous existence, primarily due to steroids and injuries on the job. I often notice the expression of someone fighting to suppress pain etched across his face. Due to his former addiction, John refuses to take anything stronger than Advil. Still, like all those mentioned before him, he remains undeterred. When a friend called about his son in a drug-induced crisis, John was ready, willing, and able to travel wherever the young man could be found.

C. S. Lewis once again enlightens us on the depth of God's love:

> To be a Christian means to forgive the inexcusable, because God has forgiven the inexcusable in you.[5]

We must do the same . . . love the unlovable just as God loves us. The truest expression of that love is forgiveness. It is upon the altar of grace that all of us may be redeemed and, in my experience, the place where God is most likely to intervene in our lives.

Endnotes

1. Michael Hallett and Byron R. Johnson, "The New Prison Ministry Lies in Bible Education," *Christianity Today*, October 19, 2021, https://www.christianitytoday.com/ct/2021/november/christian-prison-ministry-bible-education-seminary.html.

2. Aleksandr Solzhenitsyn, *The Gulag Archipelago 1918–1956: An Experiment in Literary Investigation* (New York: Harper & Row; First Edition January 1, 1975).

3. Highlights of the 2002 National Youth Gang Survey, published in 2004 by the Office of National Juvenile Justice and Delinquency Prevention (OJJDP). OJJDP Youth Gang Server, NCJ Number: 204957. https://www.ojp.gov/pdffiles1/ojjdp/fs200401.pdf.

4. From 2014 to 2017 I led a foundation (Serving California) that worked with Prison Fellowship, World Impact, and Awana Lifeline to provide inmates a three-and-a-half-year course of study, equivalent to a Bachelor's Degree in Christian Theology, known as The Urban Ministry Institute (TUMI). We followed some three hundred inmates in California prisons who participated in the classes and then paroled out of prison. Our recidivism statistic for TUMI participants was 6 percent.

5. C. S. Lewis, *The Weight of Glory* (1949; repr. ed. New York: Harper Collins, 2001), 183.